BOEING 777

LONDON G...
ATLANTA

Front cover:
Approaching the threshold at Atlanta, the pilot applies a burst of thrust to counter a loss of speed caused by windshear.

Back cover:
The 16th Boeing 777 to enter service with British Airways is parked on the Boeing flightline at Everett, Washington. BA received this aircraft, G-VIIK, a month early.

Cover, overall:
The Aerad map of the North Atlantic. *Aerad*

Above:
Boeing launched the 777 programme on 15 October 1990 after an order from United Airlines for 34 of the aircraft. This followed an intensive four-year market study by Boeing of airline requirements for a jet sized between the 767-300 and 747-400. The first 777, pictured here, flew on 12 June 1994. *Boeing*

Inset:
'Seven November, follow the 747 onto taxiway six.'

Main picture:
On the ramp at Heathrow. The first day of a long career as a commercial jetliner.

BOEING 777
LONDON GATWICK-ATLANTA

BRUCE CAMPION-SMITH

Ian Allan
PUBLISHING

Contents

First published 1999

ISBN 0 7110 2565 7

Published by Ian Allan Publishing

an imprint of Ian Allan Publishing Ltd, Terminal House, Shepperton, Surrey TW17 8AS.
Printed by Ian Allan Printing Ltd, Riverdene Business Park, Hersham, Surrey KT12 4RG.

Code: 9902/B1

Acknowledgements

A project like this may seem simple — just grab the camera and notebook, hop on the jet and go. In fact, it was only possible with the assistance of dozens of people and the wonderful support of British Airways.

Honor Verrier, the airline's Vice-President of Public Relations for North America, gave the book her backing from the start and made the introductions that got it under way. Her assistant Konnie Trainor was very helpful as well.

Kevin Mottram, the Flight Manager, Technical, of the 777 fleet at the time, gave the project his enthusiastic support and made the many arrangements to ensure its success. This book would not have been possible without his generous and kind assistance.

My thanks also to his colleague Chris Parsons, Assistant Flight Manager, Technical. I had the pleasure of meeting up with Chris and Kevin in Seattle for a 777 delivery flight to Heathrow. Both pilots patiently endured my endless questions about the operation of the 777 and for that, I am grateful. My thanks as well to Janet Bissenden, the 777 Fleet Secretary for her help.

Thank you to the Senior First Officer Graeme Lunn and First Officer Rehman Shivjee who joined Kevin on the flightdeck for British Airways Flight 2227, the trip to Atlanta that is the subject of this book.

Other British Airways staff lent their support: Barry Gosnold and Peter Jones in Seattle; Andy Patsalides; Captain Nick Feakes, training manager for the 777 fleet, for a fun and educating session in the 777 simulator; and Captains Peter Jenkinson and Phil Dunglinson for their company on a 777 flight LHR-JFK.

Thanks to the many others who assisted: Kirsti Dunn of Boeing's public relations department for her help during my visit to the Everett factory; Errol Weaver, Boeing's public relations contact in Canada; Pam and John Dibbs for a selection of terrific air-to-air images of the 777; Racal Avionics for its kind permission to reproduce airport charts and approach plates; Larry Frank of Nikon Canada for the loan of some wonderful Nikon lenses; and my colleagues Mike Slaughter and David Cooper at *The Toronto Star* for some photographic advice. The photos were taken by the author unless otherwise noted.

And thanks to Lori and David, two special people at home.

Bruce Campion-Smith
Toronto
November 1998

Excerpts in the 'En Route' chapter are reprinted with the permission of Scribner, a Division of Simon and Schuster, from *The Spirit of St Louis* by Charles Lindbergh. Copyright 1953 by Charles Scribner's Sons; copyright renewed © 1981 by Anne Morrow Lindbergh.

Opposite:
A truck pumps fuel from a hydrant system connected to the airport's fuel farm into a fuelling port on the leading edge of the left wing.

Below:
Half-way across the ocean and the flight is going smoothly and ahead of schedule.

Glossary

ACARS	Aircraft communication addressing and reporting system	MCP	Mode control panel
		MFD	Multi-function display
ADF	Automatic direction finder	MNPS	Minimum navigation performance sector
ADI	Attitude director indicator		
AGL	Above ground level	N1, N2	Engine compressor speeds expressed as a percentage
AIMS	Aircraft information management system		
		NAT	North Atlantic
APP	Approach (autopilot mode)	ND	Navigation display
APU	Auxiliary power unit	nm	nautical mile
A/T	Autothrottle	OCA	Oceanic control area
ATC	Air traffic control	PFD	Primary flight display
ATIS	Automatic terminal information service	QFE	Height above airport elevation or runway threshold based on local station atmospheric pressure
CAT I, II, III	Categories of ILS systems		
CAVOK	Ceiling and visibility okay	QNH	Altitude above sea-level based on local station atmospheric pressure
CDU	Control and display unit		
CMC	Central maintenance computer	RAT	Ram air turbine
DH	Decision height	R/T	Radiotelephony
DME	Distance measuring equipment	RTO	Rejected take-off
EFIS	Electronic flight information system	RVR	Runway visual range
		Satcom	Satellite communications
E-GPWS	Enhanced ground proximity warning system	SID	Standard instrument departure
		STAR	Standard terminal arrival route
EGT	Exhaust gas temperature	TAS	True airspeed
EICAS	Engine indication and crew alerting system	TCAS	Traffic alert and collision avoidance system
ETOPS	Extended-range, twin-engine operations	TO/GA	Take-off/Go-around buttons on throttles
FL	Flight level	UTC	Co-ordinated universal time (also known as Zulu time)
FMC	Flight management computer		
FMS	Flight management system	V1	Take-off decision speed
F/O	First Officer	V2	Take-off safety speed
fpm	feet per minute	VFR	Visual flight rules
GPS	Global positioning system	VHF	Very high frequency (radio)
HDG	Heading (autopilot mode)	VNAV	Vertical navigation (autopilot mode)
HF	High frequency		
IAS	Indicated airspeed	VOR	VHF omni-directional radio range
IFR	Instrument flight rules	VR	Rotation speed
ILS	Instrument landing system	Vref	Reference landing speed
LNAV	Lateral navigation (autopilot mode)	VSI	Vertical speed indicator
		ZFW	Zero fuel weight

Triple Seven

What seems routine for air travellers today was revolutionary back on 20 December 1957 when Boeing's first commercial jet, the 707-120, made its maiden flight.

The aircraft — the commercial version of the prototype Dash 80 jet — established the classic configuration for jetliners to come: its wings were swept back 35°; its four engines were mounted under the wings in widely separated pods so an uncontained failure in one would not damage another.

The cabin featured such innovations as folding armrests, opaque plastic window shades and cantilevered seats supported by just two sets of legs to allow space underneath to stow carry-on items.

It was not the first commercial jet on the market but it became one of the most popular. Powered by early Pratt & Whitney turbojet engines, initially it barely had the range to cross the Atlantic Ocean. But the aircraft were larger, faster and smoother than propeller aircraft and their introduction changed the face of international travel. They enabled airlines to carry more passengers at greater speeds. Air fares dropped and air travel — once reserved for the privileged classes — became more affordable. In the years since, Boeing added five more models to its family of jetliners: the 727, the company's only trijet; the 737, the best-selling jet in the world; the 747 jumbo jet, built in response to crowded airports and growing demand for travel; and the twinjets 757 and 767.

By February 1998, Boeing had delivered 8,559 jetliners. On a cool, damp day in the United States Pacific Northwest, the company was set to add to that

Below:
British Airways' initial order for 15 777s has swelled to 45. The airline uses the jet on routes to the Middle East and the United States. *John M. Dibbs*

Right:
By October 1998, 28 airlines had ordered 429 777s, demonstrating the aircraft had found a successful niche. Singapore Airlines is one of the largest 777 customers with 77 of the jets on order. *Boeing*

impressive total with the delivery of a 777, its seventh jet model and the last all-new design the company will produce this century.

Two British Airways pilots have come to the Boeing flightline in Everett, Washington, to take delivery of G-VIIK, a Boeing 777-236IGW, or Increased Gross Weight model. This will be the 16th 777 into service with the airline. Number 17 is in the paint shop and the 18th 777 for British Airways is in final assembly on the factory floor.

The delivery marks the end of years of planning and research that led the airline to order the jet and the months of construction that produced it.

The story of 'India Kilo' started seven months earlier in the summer of 1997 when the first of more than three million parts that make up the jet arrived at the factory. Over the ensuing months, components continued to flow from Boeing's 1,700 suppliers across the United States and around the globe: the wing's trailing edge panels and engine aft strut fairings from Canada; the nose section from Kansas; the rudder from Australia; dorsal fin from Brazil; radome from Italy. The massive wing centre section, built in Japan, is so large that it was sent by sea in a shipping container the size of a small house. Week by week, the pieces came together to form a 777, one of the newest and largest jets in the skies today.

But the delivery is part of a process that started long before assembly of 'India Kilo' began. It dates back to the early 1990s when British Airways embarked on its trijet replacement project. The goal was to find an aircraft smaller than the 747 for medium- and long-haul markets, a jet capable of flying the routes then being served by the airline's L-1011s and DC-10s. Under consideration were the Airbus A340, the McDonnell Douglas MD-11 and the new twin-engine design under consideration by Boeing.

A purchase decision of this magnitude is determined by a myriad of factors that include technical feasibility, price, market appeal and commonality with other aircraft in the fleet. British Airways announced in 1991 that it had ordered 15 777s — five of the -200 base model and 10 IGW models, which have greater fuel capacity and a higher maximum weight allowing them to fly longer routes.

The five base model aircraft, configured with larger first class and business class cabins, are used on routes to the Middle East: oil-rich destinations such as Riyadh, Jeddah, Dhahran, Kuwait, Muscat, Abu Dhabi and Dubai. The longer-range IGW models are flying transatlantic routes to places such as Boston, Detroit, Bermuda and Dallas.

The aircraft has proven so versatile in service that airline planners continue to order more. In August 1998, British

Airways announced a \$5-billion deal for 16 777s and took options for an additional 16, bringing its total orders for 777s to 45. Some of these 777 orders substitute existing orders for five 401-seat 747-400s. The growing number of 777s in the airline's fleet has been a factor in the airline's decision to retire 15 747-100s, starting in 1998, and its eight DC-10s the following year. In March 1998, Air France took delivery of the first of 10 777s it had on order. This aircraft was delivered with a new maximum take-off weight of 294,192kg and because of this, it carries the designation 'ER' for 'extended range' rather than 'IGW'. The latest 777s ordered by British Airways will be even heavier with a maximum take-off weight of 297,824kg and, as a result, they have been given the nickname 'ER-plus'. Because of this higher gross weight, British Airways also switched from the GE90 engine, which powers its existing fleet of 777s, and chose the more powerful Rolls-Royce Trent 895 engine, which offers 93,000lb of thrust. These 777-200ERs will be capable of flying up to 256 passengers and more than 16 tonnes of cargo nonstop on all but ultra-long routes. They were ordered as a replacement for the 747-200. By the end of 1998, British Airways had taken delivery of 19 777s and 10 more were to be delivered in 1999. Deliveries of the heavier-model 777s will begin in January 2000 and continue to 2002.

The traits that made the 707 a good airliner are found on the 777 — the podded underwing engines, the sweptback wing, the same attention to cabin design. And like its predecessor four decades earlier, the 777 breaks new ground.

THE AIRCRAFT

The 777 is a remarkable aircraft. It has the economy of a twin yet, in its stretched version, also has the range and passenger capacity to replace older 747 models. But the 777 is much more than a new jetliner. For Boeing, it launched a new philosophy and a new way to build aircraft.

Boeing originally intended its new jet to be a stretched derivative of the 767 but those plans went nowhere in the face of a lukewarm response from the airlines. The carriers were clear in their demands: they wanted a wide-body aircraft with the efficiencies of the 767 but able to carry more passengers longer distances, something that could replace the hundreds of ageing three- and four-engined jets. For example, Cathay Pacific Airways needed a replacement for its L-1011s and in

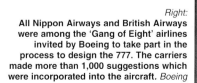

Right:
All Nippon Airways and British Airways were among the 'Gang of Eight' airlines invited by Boeing to take part in the process to design the 777. The carriers made more than 1,000 suggestions which were incorporated into the aircraft. *Boeing*

1988 United Airlines was shopping around to replace its workhorse, the DC-10. Boeing designers were forced back to the drawing board to develop an aircraft that would fit between the 269-seat 767-300 and the 420-seat 747-400.

Boeing then took the unusual step of asking the airlines to help decide the features of the new jet. It convened what became known as the 'Gang of Eight' and invited planners from United Airlines, American Airlines, Delta Air Lines, British Airways, Japan Airlines, All Nippon Airways, Cathay Pacific Airways and Qantas Airways to take part in the design process. There was no question that Boeing built good aircraft. But the airlines contributed the lessons they learned in operating jets 10hr a day in every season and every kind of weather. They brought in their own experts — mechanics told Boeing how to make the plane easier to maintain and flight attendants told Boeing how to improve the galleys and overall passenger service.

When the consultations were over, Boeing and the airlines had decided the make-up of the new jet: the cabin would have near-747 dimensions, wide enough to seat passengers 9- or 10-abreast; it would incorporate technological advances like fly-by-wire flight controls, an advanced digital flightdeck and make extensive use of weight-saving composites. It would seat between 305 and 440 passengers depending on configuration and would be offered at gross weights from 229,520 to 286,900kg. It would have flexibility in range, routes and interior configurations — a jet that could be used on high-density domestic routes as well as long over-water flights that had been the domain of three- and four-engine aircraft.

Right:
The 777 was rolled out on 9 April 1994.
Boeing

Below:
The first delivery of a 777 was to United Airlines on 17 May 1995 during a ceremony at Seattle's Museum of Flight marked by a flypast of the first 777.
Boeing

Above:
The first Boeing 777 taxies down the main runway at Paine Field in Everett Washington. The Boeing factory and flightline are visible in the background. The building, already the biggest in the world by volume, was enlarged another 50% — from 25 hectares to 39 hectares — to accommodate the production line for the 777. *Boeing*

Right:
In early 1998, Boeing was producing seven 777s a month. Shown here in the final assembly area is the 18th 777 for British Airways.

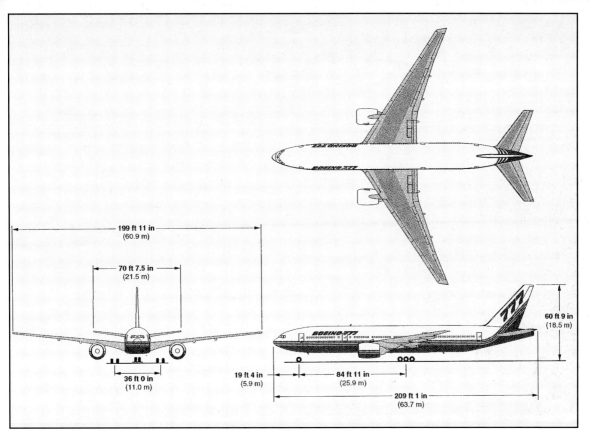

Dimensions shown in figure:
- 199 ft 11 in (60.9 m)
- 70 ft 7.5 in (21.5 m)
- 36 ft 0 in (11.0 m)
- 19 ft 4 in (5.9 m)
- 84 ft 11 in (25.9 m)
- 209 ft 1 in (63.7 m)
- 60 ft 9 in (18.5 m)

Above:
The general arrangement of the 777. *Boeing*

The programme got the green light in October 1990 after United Airlines ordered 34 Pratt & Whitney-powered 777-200s and placed options for 34 more. British Airways placed its order in August 1991 and in a move that was not without controversy, announced its 777s would be powered by the GE90, an all-new engine from General Electric, rather than the Rolls-Royce Trent 800.

With the jet launched, four airlines — United, All Nippon, British Airways and Japan Airlines — remained involved to influence the aircraft's design. British Airways pushed for an increase in the maximum take-off weight to 242,675kg from 233,600kg for the initial 777 design. The airline also suggested changing the arrangement of the rear galley to make space for two lavatories from elsewhere in the plane. Moving the lavatories aft opened up room for four more seats.

In addition to this unprecedented involvement of the airlines, the design of the 777 was unique in another fashion — it was designed entirely on computer without blueprints or the traditional full-scale wood and metal mock-up used on past designs to confirm parts fit properly. Instead, the parts for the 777 were preassembled on computer, creating a digital mock-up of the aircraft which revealed any problems before production.

The first 777 flew on 12 June 1994 and first delivery to United Airlines took place almost a year later on 17 May 1995.

Boeing offers three versions of the 777: the base model 777-200; the 777-200IGW; and the stretched 777-300 which can seat up to 550 passengers in an all-economy configuration.

The maximum gross weight of the base model ranges from 229,520kg to 247,210kg with engines rated at 74,000 to 77,000lb thrust. It can carry 31,000gal of fuel, allowing flights between the US East Coast and Europe. It seats 305 to 328 passengers in a three-class arrangement, or 375-400 in two classes.

British Airways was the launch customer for the IGW model. It has the same dimensions as the base model but has higher maximum take-off weights of 263,080kg to 286,900kg using engines rated at 84,700lb and 90,000lb thrust. This variant also has a larger centre tank, allowing it to carry a total of 45,220gal of fuel, 14,220gal more than the base model. It can fly routes of 5,960nm to 7,230nm, enough for nonstop flights between city pairs such as London and Los Angeles and Tokyo and Sydney. This version, which first flew in October 1996, has proved to be the most popular model of the 777 series. The first IGW aircraft was delivered to British Airways in February 1997.

In September 1997, Boeing rolled out the world's longest commercial jetliner — the 777-300. Two fuselage plugs extend the -300 model to just over 242ft, 33ft longer than the -200 model and even longer than the 747-400. As a result, the capacity of the big jet is

Above:
The 777 has a feature that makes it unique among Boeing jetliners — a perfectly round fuselage. This makes for a spacious cabin and generous cargo holds.
British Airways

Right:
The 777's range out of London for both the base model and the increased gross weight variant.
Boeing

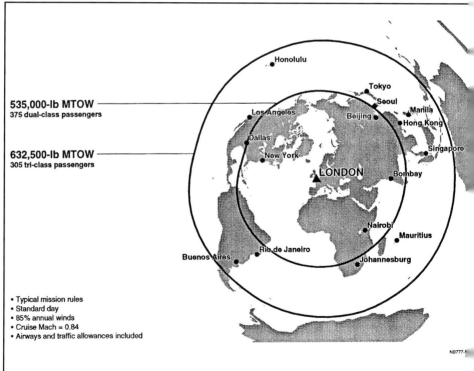

535,000-lb MTOW
305 tri-class passengers

632,500-lb MTOW
375 dual-class passengers

Honolulu
Tokyo
Seoul
Los Angeles
Beijing
Manila
Hong Kong
Dallas
New York
Singapore
LONDON
Bombay
Nairobi
Mauritius
Rio de Janeiro
Buenos Aires
Johannesburg

• Typical mission rules
• Standard day
• 85% annual winds
• Cruise Mach = 0.84
• Airways and traffic allowances included

NB777-5

Above:
The 777-300 takes to the air for the first time on 16 October 1997. This version of the 777 has been extended by 33ft to 242ft 4in, making it longer than the 747.
Boeing

increased by about 20% to seat 328 to 394 passengers in a three-class arrangement, or 400 to 479 in two classes. With a fuel capacity of 45,220gal, the same as the IGW model, the 777-300 has a range of 5,700nm and a maximum take-off weight of 299,370kg. The range and seating capacity of the -300 make it an ideal replacement for older model 747s, with big savings in fuel and maintenance.

Dubbed the 'people mover' because of its size, the 777-300 best serves the high capacity, medium-length routes. It is no surprise then that this model is selling well among Asian carriers such as All Nippon Airways, Korean Air and Thai Airways International. The 777-300 received type certification and approval for 180min extended-range, twin-engine operations on 4 May 1998. It was the first time any aircraft manufacturer had received both approvals on the same day. Launch customer Cathay Pacific took delivery later that month of the first of seven 777-300s it has on order for use on high frequency regional routes.

Key to the growth of the 777 is its huge wing which can handle increases in gross weight up to 326,592kg. Several other 777 variants are under study to take advantage of this: the smaller 777-100X, an ultra long-range model that could fly farther than the 747-400; and the 777-200X, which would combine the longer range of the -100X with the larger capacity of the -200.

The 777-200X would have a maximum take-off weight of between 312,984kg and 326,592kg and be powered by 98,000lb thrust engines. A fuel capacity of 46,680gal would give it the ability to carry 305 passengers about 8,500nm.

Boeing was also considering a 'shrink' of the 777-200, called the -100X, to serve very long range routes. The aircraft would be 21ft shorter than the 777-200 but operating at 299,375kg, the -100 would carry 250 passengers 8,500nm, enough to permit nonstop flights between virtually any two cities.

Also under evaluation was the -300X, a heavier version of the 777-300 that would carry extra fuel to increase the jet's range to more than 6,500nm.

By 30 September 1998, 156 777s were flying worldwide and Boeing had orders for 382 777-200s, IGW and ER models, and another 47 for the 777-300.

THE FLIGHTDECK

The 'Working Together' theme that characterised the development of the Boeing 777 did not stop at the flightdeck door. When it came time to design the cockpit, Boeing relied heavily on the suggestions of nearly 700 industry and airline pilots who logged several thousand hours in a 777 simulator, even before the jetliner itself had been built.

The result is a traditional, two-crew flightdeck that builds on the glass cockpit technology pioneered with the 757 and 767 and later improved on in the 747-400. Pilots appreciate even the small touches on the 777, like the larger, easier to read lettering on the instrument panels, the convenient locations of the cup holders, pencil holders, clipboards and writing surfaces, and the master brightness control. By turning a single knob on the overhead panel, either pilot can adjust the brightness of the display and panel lighting.

In front of each pilot are two 8in square displays, similar to the layout of the 747-400, which present the information needed to fly and navigate the jet. These displays are advanced liquid crystal displays (LCD) which are smaller, lighter and generate less heat than the cathode ray tubes they replace. The LCDs are also easier to read in a variety of lighting conditions, from night-time to direct sunlight.

The Primary Flight Display (PFD) located directly in front of each pilot incorporates the flying instruments such as airspeed and altitude on one screen for easy viewing.

The Navigation Display (ND) is located inboard of the PFD and can be selected to present navigation information in a variety of formats. Typically, the ND is left in MAP mode which depicts 80° of compass rose across the top with the jet's current heading highlighted in a box. Below that, a moving map shows the programmed waypoints with the aircraft symbol at the bottom. The crew can select ranges from 10nm for navigation during departure and arrival up to 640nm for en route navigation. At the touch of a button, the pilots can call up a variety of information on the ND, such as the location of airports and radio beacons. Returns from the weather radar can be overlaid on the map display to help the crew avoid severe weather.

Two other displays are set one above the other in the centre panel. The top display is used for the engine indication and crew alerting system (EICAS) and shows the fuel quantity, position of flaps and landing gear and other information including warning, caution and advisory messages. This display also shows the two primary engine indications: N1 fan speed and the exhaust gas temperature (EGT). N1 is used as the main reference for setting power on the GE90, unlike the Pratt & Whitney and Rolls-Royce engines which use engine pressure ratio (EPR) as the primary guide. Gear and flap indications are at the bottom right and appear only when the gear or flaps are down or are in transit.

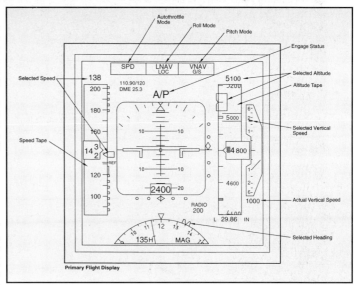

Right:
In front of each pilot are the Primary Flight Display (PFD) and Navigation Display (ND). The PFD, seen here, incorporates the flying instruments on one screen for easy viewing. Boeing

Below right:
The Navigation Display (ND) can be selected to present navigation information in a variety of formats. Boeing

Primary Flight Display

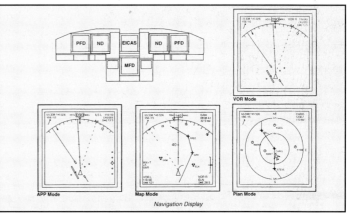

Navigation Display

The crew alerting function continuously monitors aircraft systems and displays a message if a fault occurs. Depending how serious the fault is, a chime may also sound and the master warning or caution lights illuminate. The messages are divided into several categories. Warnings are for conditions that require immediate action, like an engine fire. These are displayed in red and are accompanied by the master warning lights on the glareshield and an aural alert, such as a bell, automated voice or siren. Caution messages are shown in amber for conditions that are not urgent but require some action by the crew, such as low oil pressure. These activate the master caution lights and a beeper. To avoid distracting the pilots on take-off, the master warning lights and fire bell are inhibited from V1 to 400ft above ground. Other alerts are inhibited starting at 80kt until the aircraft is safely airborne. Likewise, some warnings are inhibited on approach from 200ft above ground until the aircraft has landed and slowed below 75kt. Advisories, also shown in amber, are the least urgent. Memos, shown in white, are reminders to the crew about the status of certain manually selected items, such as the no smoking signs or parking brake. The aircraft even keeps watch over the crew's alertness by monitoring the activation of switches on the mode control panel, radios and other functions. If too long a time passes since the last activity, it generates the EICAS advisory 'PILOT RESPONSE'. If this fails to spark pilot action, it upgrades to a caution message and then a warning, each time with all the associated aural alerts and lights.

Below the EICAS display and just ahead of the throttles, is the multi-function display (MFD). This is used to present secondary engine information, such as N2 compressor speeds, oil temperatures and pressures, engine vibrations and fuel flow. Using a selector located on the right side of the glareshield, the pilots can also call up synoptic diagrams showing the status of flight controls, landing gear, cabin and cargo doors and the fuel, hydraulic, electrical and environmental control systems. The flight control synoptic page, for example, shows the movement of all primary flight controls — ailerons, spoilers, elevators and rudder. Other synoptic pages reveal such information as the brake temperatures

— important after an aborted take-off — the position of fuel valves and the output of electrical generators. This lower screen is typically kept dark but should a problem occur, the pilots will get an alert and can display the synoptic of the system in question. To the right of the EICAS display are the landing gear selector handle, alternate gear controls and autobrake selector. On the left side of the screen are three LCD standby instruments for attitude, airspeed and altitude.

Two additional displays located on the outboard sides of the cockpit are used by the crew to get reports on the aircraft's technical operation, like engine performance in many more parameters than shown on the EICAS. Eventually, it is expected these displays will be used for an electronic library containing on-line the many aircraft manuals, charts and books now stowed around the flightdeck.

The glareshield above the instrument panel contains the master warning and caution lights and the mode control panel for the autopilot, autothrottle and flight directors. Typically, the autopilot is used in LNAV (lateral navigation) and VNAV (vertical navigation) modes for best efficiency but, alternatively, the autopilot can be selected to maintain a target airspeed or Mach speed, a heading or track, a vertical speed or flightpath

angle, and altitude. When the track feature is activated, the autopilot will automatically fly a heading while correcting for wind. This is useful when flying a non-precision approach.

Also located on the glareshield are two para-visual devices (PVD), one in front of each pilot, which provide directional guidance during low-visibility take-offs. Looking like a black and white barber's pole turned on its side, the stripes rotate towards the centreline of the runway, giving the pilots an easy and intuitive 'follow me' reference when they may see only one or two runway lights out the cockpit window. With the PVD, take-offs are permitted in visibility as low as 75m. Without it, the take-off minimum is doubled to 150m.

The centre console contains the thrust levers, the speedbrake lever, parking brake, flap lever and behind the throttles, the fuel control switches. Further back on the console are the controls for the weather radar and transponder, aileron and rudder trim, the engine fire extinguisher panel and the frequency selectors for the VHF and HF radios. The crew use a control display unit at the rear of the centre console to handle the functions of the satellite communications system. The satcom system uses satellites to relay voice and data communications to ground stations when out of VHF range. It is unaffected by the atmospheric disturbances which make HF radios now in use unintelligible at times.

The aircraft is also equipped with ACARS, the Aircraft Communication Addressing and Reporting System. This datalink system sends information between an aircraft and an airline ground base, allowing pilots easy communications for dispatch and weather updates. Using the keyboard, the pilots type in messages which are then transmitted to airline operations staff and air traffic control. Hard copies of ACARS messages are obtained from a printer at the rear of the console.

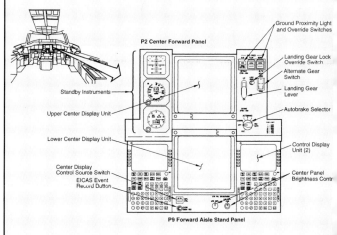

Top:
The PFD and ND on approach to Runway 27 Right at Heathrow. The PFD shows the jet descending at 950fpm, just slightly below the ILS glideslope. The A/P indicates the autopilot is engaged. The aircraft is flying at 180kt and note the flap speeds displayed on the airspeed tape. The selected ILS frequency and DME read-out are shown on the upper left. On the ND, the aircraft position is indicated by the white triangle.

Above:
In the centre of the instrument panel is the display for the engine indication and crew alerting system (EICAS). Below it are the multi-function display and two control display units used to access the flight management computer.
Boeing

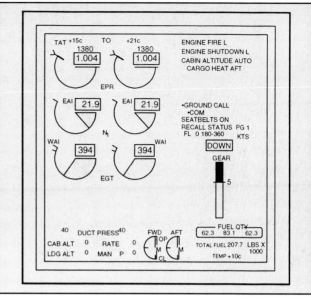

Left:
The EICAS display in the centre of the instrument panel shows the primary engine instrumentation, warning and alert messages, the position of the flaps and gear. On the left are the back-up instruments; the gear handle is on the right.

Above:
A typical presentation on the EICAS panel. *Boeing*

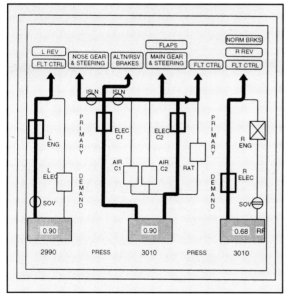

Above:
Synoptics showing the status of various aircraft systems can be called up on the multi-function display located just ahead of the throttles. Here is the hydraulic system synoptic. *Boeing*

Above right:
Maintenance information can be called up on these sidewall displays.

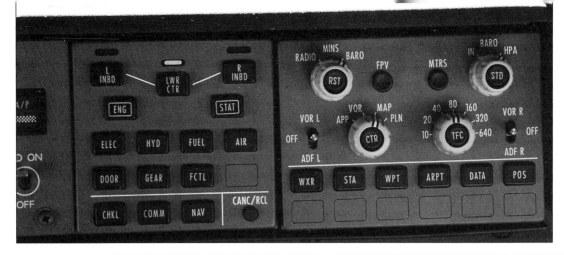

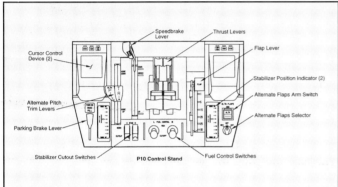

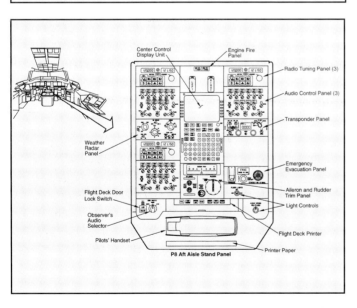

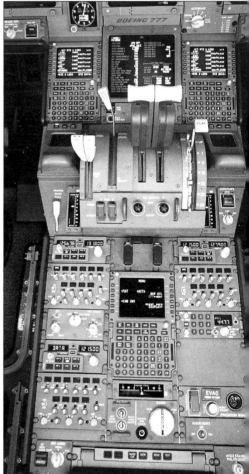

Centre
The control stand.
Boeing

Above:
The centre console.
Boeing

Top:
At each end of the glareshield are the control panels for the electronic flight instrument system (EFIS).

The pilots control most of the flight using the Flight Management Computer System (FMC) which is accessed through three full-colour multipurpose control display units, or CDUs, on the centre console. The FMC is programmed through these keyboard units for such tasks as navigation and to determine and set V-speeds and engine derates for take-off.

At the start of each flight, the crew programme the FMC with details of the routeing. The flight management computer has a database with details of the 777's performance such as drag and engine characteristics, maximum and optimum altitudes, maximum and minimum speeds. The FMC uses the flightplan details together with this database to compute an optimum flight profile that balances speed and economy. It then sends the pitch, roll and thrust commands required to fly this profile to the autopilot, autothrottle and flight directors. The FMC will automatically fly the programmed route when the autopilot is set to LNAV mode. Likewise, when VNAV is selected it will fly the jet on the most efficient climb, cruise and descent profiles.

The computer's navigational database, updated every 28 days, contains information on VORs — including frequencies and identifiers — waypoints, airways, airports, runways, departure and arrival procedures and company flightplans. At the push of a few buttons, the pilots can tell their bearing and distance from virtually any radio beacon, waypoint or airport in the world.

The flight management computer is a function of an advanced avionics system known as the Aircraft Information Management System (AIMS) made by Honeywell. What makes the system unique is that it is contained in a single cabinet in the main equipment centre below and just aft of the flightdeck. (The 777 has two identical AIMS cabinets for redundancy.) In other aircraft, each of these functions is done in separate line replaceable units (LRU), resulting in considerable duplication of hardware and software common to all the units.

Opposite:
The control stand and centre console contain the thrust levers, the speedbrake lever, parking brake and flap lever. Further back on the console are the controls for the weather radar and transponder, trim settings, engine fire extinguishers and frequency selectors for the VHF and HF radios.

Below:
A new feature on the 777 are the electronic checklists that are called up on the multi-function display. The individual items on the list turn from white to green when completed. Displayed here is the checklist for a fire in the left engine.

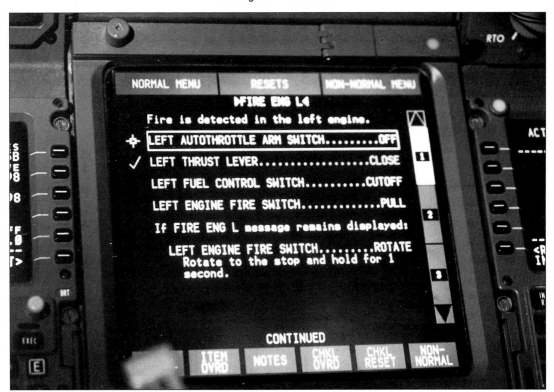

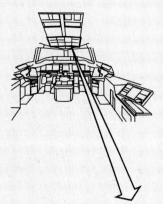

1. Air Data Inertial Reference System Control
2. Primary Flight Computers Disconnect
3. Electrical System/APU
4. Wiper Control
5. Emergency Lighting
6. Passenger Oxygen
7. Window Heat
8. Ram Air Turbine Switch
9. Hydraulic System
10. Passenger Signs

11. APU and Cargo Fire Control
12. Engine Start
13. Fuel Jettison
14. Fuel Management
15. Anti-ice
16. Air Conditioning
17. Bleed Air
18. Pressurization
19. Lighting

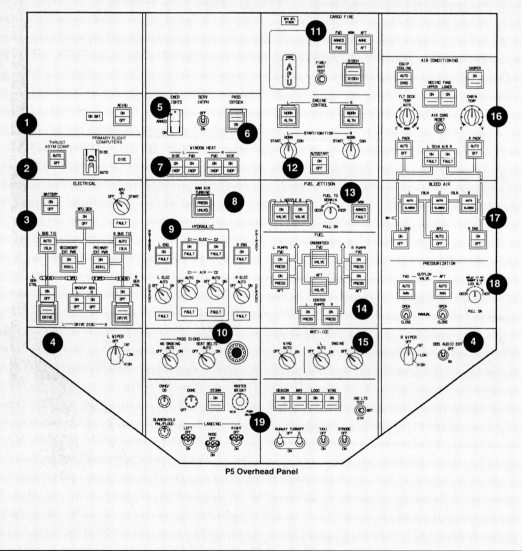

P5 Overhead Panel

Another important AIMS function is the central maintenance computer system. An upgrade of the system installed on the 747-400, this computer collects detailed data on aircraft systems and components such as fuel, electrical, flight controls and hydraulics. The result is easier trouble-shooting and reduced downtime chasing elusive faults. Maintenance crews can access the system on the flightdeck using a computer terminal behind the first officer's seat.

The 777 navigates precisely without reference to ground-based navigation aids using a sophisticated unit made by Honeywell called ADIRS which combines the functions of air data sensing and inertial reference. At the heart of the unit are six accelerometers and six ring-laser gyros which could fit in the palm of a hand. Lasers are beamed in opposite directions through the triangular gyros, reflected off mirrors in each corner. When the aircraft attitude changes, the light beams are minutely affected. A computer detects and measures the differences among several gyros to determine even the slightest change in the aircraft's position. As well, a twin global positioning system (GPS) is now installed as basic equipment. The GPS receivers use signals from a network of 24 satellites to fix the jet's position with remarkable precision, including its altitude above sea level. The FMC combines the signals from all navigation aids — the ring-laser gyros and VOR and DME signals — but typically uses the GPS system as the main source of position information because of the pinpoint accuracy of the satellite system.

The aircraft is equipped with the usual complement of navigation radios such as VOR, DME and ILS which are normally tuned automatically by the flight management computer for FMC updating and flying approaches. The identifier of the VOR or ILS is shown on the PFD or ND. The crew can manually tune navigation radios including ADFs on the NAV/RAD page of the CDU.

One helpful feature of the 777 is its electronic checklists. Normal and non-normal checklists can be called up on the MFD. The avionics system senses the position of many switches, controls and other data and automatically indicates completed items. The checklists are controlled using two cursor control devices located just ahead of the throttles on either side of the centre console. The pilots use these touch-sensitive pads to move the cursor around the displays and scroll through items on the checklist.

The overhead panel has the controls for major aircraft systems like fuel, electrical and hydraulic systems as well as pressurisation, bleed air and the auxiliary

power unit (APU). It also contains the switches for exterior lights, anti-icing and windshield wipers which are rarely used because the windscreens are treated with a rain repellent.

The traditional look of the flightdeck hides a feature of the 777 that makes it unique among Boeing jetliners — a fly-by-wire (FBW) flight control system.

In a conventional aircraft, cables are used to transmit a pilot's commands to the rudder, ailerons, flaps and slats. In a fly-by-wire design, the movements of the control column and rudder pedals are converted to electrical signals and transmitted through computers and electrical wires to the control surfaces. These computers use information from other aircraft systems — air data, flap and slat positions and engine thrust, for example — to calculate the proper commands for roll, pitch and yaw, resulting in enhanced handling. The 777's FBW system includes a number of built-in protections to deter a pilot from flying the jet outside its normal operating envelope — banking the aircraft too steeply or going too slow or too fast. But in keeping with Boeing's design philosophy, these safeguards can be overridden, leaving the final authority with the flight crew. For example, in a turn greater than 35° bank, bank angle protection requires additional force on the control

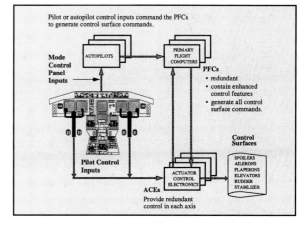

Pilot or autopilot control inputs command the PFCs to generate control surface commands.

Mode Control Panel Inputs

AUTOPILOTS

PRIMARY FLIGHT COMPUTERS

PFCs
• redundant
• contain enhanced control features
• generate all control surface commands.

Pilot Control Inputs

ACTUATOR CONTROL ELECTRONICS

ACEs
Provide redundant control in each axis

Control Surfaces

SPOILERS
AILERONS
FLAPERONS
ELEVATORS
RUDDER
STABILIZER

Opposite:
The overhead panel has the controls for the aircraft systems. *Boeing*

Above right:
The 777's fly-by-wire flight control system. *British Airways*

Right:
The switches on the overhead panel are within easy reach of either pilot.

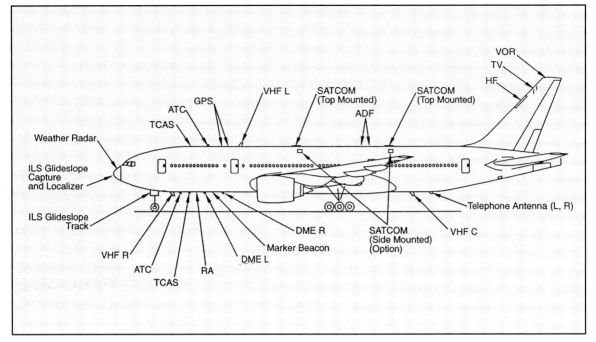

column to maintain altitude and bank angle. Should the pilot release the control column at this point, the FBW system will smartly roll the wings level. In more gentle turns — no more than 30° — a feature called turn compensation automatically applies back pressure and trims to maintain constant altitude. If the aircraft is flown too slow or too fast, the control forces increase substantially and the system will not allow the pilot to trim below a minimum safe speed or above the maximum operating speed.

The logic of Boeing's FBW system means trimming is required only for changes of airspeed. The system automatically retrims the aircraft to compensate for pitch changes that occur when flaps, spoilers and gear are extended or retracted or the thrust setting is changed.

The FBW system has a normal mode and two back-ups to ensure redundancy. In the first back-up mode, known as secondary, control of the aircraft remains the same except for the loss of the autopilot and some envelope protection functions. The second back-up, called direct mode, is used in the event of a more serious failure. The flight computers are bypassed and pilot commands go directly to the flight controls. Handling remains quite good.

In the unlikely event of a complete failure of the FBW system, the 777 is equipped with mechanical back-up cables to the stabiliser and selected spoilers to give the crew some measure of control to keep the aircraft straight and level until they sort out the problem.

Unlike the Airbus design, the control columns and throttles on the 777 move to provide the pilots with visual cues of the autopilot and autothrottle operation.

The aircraft has three sophisticated avionics systems to protect it from severe weather, a mid-air collision and the most common and deadly cause of accidents — colliding with terrain.

The ground proximity warning system is several warning systems in one, all designed to prevent the pilots from inadvertently flying an airworthy aircraft into the ground.

The system, which dates from the early 1970s, uses information from the radio altimeter and onboard systems to monitor altitude, airspeed and vertical speed. Using this data, the system becomes active within 2,500ft above ground level to alert the pilots to undesirable trends such as excessive descent rate; inadvertent descent after take-off or go-around; unsafe terrain clearance when not in landing configuration; and deviating below the glideslope on approach.

Before 1975, there was an average of eight a year of these accidents, known as controlled flight into terrain (CFIT). That rate has dropped to about four crashes a year now that ground proximity warning systems are installed on most commercial aircraft. Still, these accidents — which usually occur in clouds or darkness — remain the leading cause of fatal airline crashes, accounting for 25% of worldwide commercial air accidents from 1987 to 1996. That is due in part to several shortfalls of the current system. First, radio altimeters can only look down and cannot sense the ground ahead of the aircraft. This means the system can only provide very short warning times in fast-rising terrain. Also, to avoid nuisance alerts, terrain warnings are suspended when an aircraft is on approach with a normal descent rate and has gear and flaps deployed.

These shortcomings have led to the enhanced ground proximity warning system (E-GPWS) from AlliedSignal which has two breakthrough features: look-ahead terrain alerting and terrain display.

E-GPWS tracks an aircraft's altitude from the altimeter and its position using the GPS or inertial reference systems and compares this with information contained in a global terrain database. The computer is constantly searching the database along the aircraft's projected flightpath, providing look-ahead warning capability, even during manoeuvres. If the aircraft is descending, for example, the system searches down a sloping flightpath.

Because it can foresee potential conflicts, it sounds the alert that high ground is ahead long before the old system ever could, usually about a minute or more compared with just 10 to 15sec. The pilots first get an aural alert: 'Caution, terrain'. Twenty to 30sec from projected impact, the warning escalates to 'Terrain! Terrain! Pull up,' and the words 'PULL UP' appear on the PFDs. Getting a warning like this is serious business and calls for immediate action. The pilot would disconnect the autopilot and autothrottle, apply maximum thrust and pull the control column back to attain a pitch attitude of 20°.

In addition to more timely warnings, another benefit of the new system is it allows pilots to 'see' the terrain ahead of them. A display of the terrain around the aircraft can be selected by the crew or is automatically shown on the ND when the system detects a potential conflict. Looking much like the weather radar display, E-GPWS displays terrain using different colours — green for ground below the aircraft's altitude, yellow if about even and red if well above. Of course, the best way for pilots to avoid such an unpleasant encounter with terra firma is to maintain situational awareness and know where the aircraft is at all times.

British Airways took delivery of its first 777 with E-GPWS in March 1998. This was also the first Boeing jet equipped with the technology. (That same aircraft was also equipped with the new predictive windshear system.) The airline became the first carrier outside the United States to announce a fleet-wide retrofit to install E-GPWS on the jets it was already flying.

Another safety system onboard the aircraft is designed to prevent collisions of a different sort — with other aircraft. Called the traffic alert and collision avoidance system (TCAS), it presents pilots with a display of aircraft around them and when necessary provides audible warnings and guidance to climb or descend to avoid a mid-air collision.

The system relies on the transponders and encoding altimeters installed on commercial aircraft which transmit their positions and altitudes to air traffic control radar. In similar fashion, the TCAS equipment onboard an aircraft sends out radio signals called interrogations that trigger a response from transponders on nearby aircraft. From the information it gets back, the system determines the position of other aircraft and whether there is a threat of collision. On the 777, the position of other aircraft is displayed on the ND along with their relative altitude above or below.

If the system detects another aircraft getting too close, it issues a traffic advisory to the pilots within 48sec of a possible collision. An automated voice calls 'Traffic, Traffic' and the symbol for the other aircraft on the ND changes shape and colour. If both aircraft continue on a collision course, the pilots get a more urgent resolution advisory. The aircraft symbol changes to a solid red block and the voice commands an avoidance manoeuvre such as 'Climb, climb'. As well, directions are displayed on the PFD telling the crew whether to climb, descend or level off to avoid the other aircraft. The manoeuvres are gentle and generally not noticed by passengers.

Below:
The fuselage structure of the 777. *Boeing*

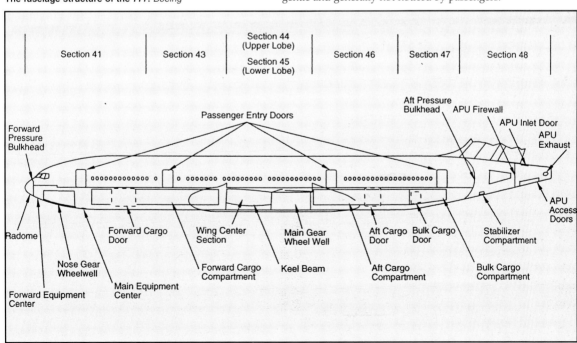

Scheduled airlines flying in the US have been required to have the TCAS system on aircraft with more than 30 passenger seats since 1994. Since then, it has prevented several mid-air collisions. One shortcoming, however, is that it cannot detect aircraft not equipped with a transponder.

New technology has also been developed to give improved warnings of a potentially deadly weather phenomenon called windshear. Most commercial aircraft are equipped with a reactive windshear warning system which warns of degraded performance only after a jet has encountered the windshear.

Until now, these dangerous air currents were invisible. But starting in 1998, 777s have been equipped with a forward-looking, predictive windshear detection system that allows pilots to avoid dangerous conditions altogether or begin recovery measures much sooner. The system uses Doppler radar to detect a rapid change in wind speed or direction in the air 3nm ahead of the aircraft. If not already turned on, the weather radar automatically turns on at 2,300ft AGL to give coverage for the approach. It also turns on before take-off to provide alerts during the roll and climbout. At typical approach speeds, the radar gives an alert 10 to 70sec before a windshear encounter. Analysis of past windshear accidents shows that in most incidents, this new system would have alerted the flight crew 20 to 40sec before an encounter, enough time for an avoidance manoeuvre. The flight crew would first hear an automated voice calling 'Monitor radar display' and the NDs would show the area of detected windshear. If the aircraft was on take-off and continued toward the windshear, the pilots would hear 'Windshear ahead'. On approach, they would hear 'Go around, windshear ahead'. If the jet flies into the windshear and suffers a loss in performance, the aural warning 'Windshear, windshear, windshear' would sound. In all three scenarios, the master warning light illuminates and the word 'WINDSHEAR' appears in red on the NDs and PFDs.

THE DELIVERY

G-VIIK sits on the flightline at Paine Field, near the sprawling factory which is home to the production lines of all Boeing's wide-body aircraft — the 747, 767 and 777.

Taking delivery of a new jet is not a simple matter of jumping in, starting the engines and flying away. Captains Kevin Mottram and Chris Parsons arrived in

Seattle six days prior to delivery day to give the 777 a thorough examination. Kevin is the Flight Manager, Technical, for British Airways' 777 fleet and Chris is the Assistant Flight Manager, Technical. Together they look after the myriad of technical details surrounding the 777's operation with the airline. This includes looking after the deliveries and a multitude of other duties like writing and updating operations manuals, acting as the liaison between flight operations and engineering departments and checking out the legal and practical considerations of launching 777 service to new destinations. In addition to these extensive tasks, both pilots like to log some line flying every month.

Their first job on a delivery is a walk-around of the aircraft. But where a normal exterior inspection before a revenue flight takes 20min, 'The Walk', as a delivery walk-around is known, starts in the morning and stretches through the day and sometimes into the evening. It is a detailed inspection of the interior and exterior of the aircraft, including several hours of systems tests on the flightdeck. All the access panels are opened and the nooks and crannies examined, safety equipment is checked installed in the cabin — they even check that labels are stuck on in the proper place.

Usually the inspection turns up only minor snags and the one on this aircraft is no exception, paving the way for a 4hr test flight the next day. The aircraft has already been flown twice by Boeing's own pilots and once on an FAA certification flight. But this upcoming test flight, called C-1, will be the first time the airline's own pilots will fly the jet. This gruelling flight puts the aircraft through its paces on normal and non-normal procedures and a test of all the back-up systems that can be safely tested in the air.

The drill starts at 39,000ft where the pilots ensure the thrust settings are within the performance specifications and check the operation of the fuel jettison system. The jet can dump two tonnes of fuel a minute. Each engine is shut down and then relit using a windmill start. Next they check the operation of the pressurisation system and de-pressurise the cabin to test the deployment of the oxygen masks. Pins are inserted to prevent the masks from fully deploying, saving the headache of having to repack all the compartments. Ten masks are allowed to

Right:
Delivery day. G-VIIK, the 16th 777 into service with British Airways, is parked on the factory flightline at Everett. The production problems which plagued other Boeing models in 1997 and 1998 did not affect the 777 line. In fact, British Airways received this 777 almost a month early.

drop free and checked for proper oxygen flow. Descending to 15,000ft, the crew slow the aircraft to near-stall speeds in both the clean and dirty configurations to check the operation of warning systems like the stick shaker. Both engines are again shut down and powered up again, this time using the starter motors. The landing gear is deployed using the alternative gear extension as would be required in case of a hydraulic failure. This procedure unlocks the landing gear and the gear doors and allows the wheels to drop into position by their own weight.

Once the upper air work is done, the crew visit Moses Lake airport in central Washington state for several touch-and-go landings, a low-level go-around, an autoland and a simulated engine-out approach. On the return flight to Paine Field, they switch off the electrical generators one by one until only a small car-sized battery is powering a few flightdeck instruments. A few seconds after the power loss, the ram air turbine (RAT) automatically deploys from a fairing behind the right wheel well. The slipstream turns the turbine's 3.5ft propeller which powers a generator that can supply 7.5kVA of electricity to aircraft systems. The APU then automatically starts up to restore all power. The crew do a similar test of the hydraulic system, shutting down the three systems that power many aircraft functions, including the flight controls. Back-up pressure is supplied by the RAT which also has a hydraulic pump. In this mode, control responses are sluggish because not all the control surfaces are powered but it is enough for the pilots to retain control. The flight ends at Paine Field with a take-off aborted above 100kt to test the automatic activation of maximum braking.

The flight is a rare demonstration of the many redundancies Boeing has built into the 777's systems; enough that a single failure, a rare happening in itself, is really a non-event.

Below:
Leaving the factory, 777s are towed to one of the paint shops to be painted in the livery of the carrier that will fly them. The jets are then moved to the flightline where they undergo several weeks of additional work, systems tests and inspections in preparation for the first flight by Boeing test pilots. Here 777s belonging to Saudi Arabian Airlines and China Southern await fitting of their engines. China Southern was the first airline to operate the 777 across the Pacific with a service between Los Angeles and Guangzhou, China.

Above:
Night flight. British Airways' new 777 flies through the darkness from Seattle to Heathrow on a route that takes it across Canada and Greenland. Captain Kevin Mottram passes the time with regular checks of the jet's progress.

On this aircraft, Kevin and Chris note the recurrence of a troublesome bug with the fly-by-wire power supply. The problem is rooted in the back-up battery that is designed to ensure there is no break in power to the flight control system when, for example, the power supply switches from the APU to the engine generators. For some reason, the battery is draining away. With all the redundancies built into the 777, this is not a safety concern. But because the health of the battery is a go/no-go item, it can snarl a flight. A previously delivered 777 had the same problem and caused British Airways all sorts of grief. For that reason, Kevin was understandably irked when he got an EICAS message during the test flight informing him this aircraft had a similar problem.

The days following the test flight are spent rectifying the few small problems that have been uncovered and working on the snag with the FBW battery.

On delivery day, the pilots go to the Boeing delivery centre, a single-storey building on the flightline. The ramp is bustling with activity as 767s, 747-400s and 777s are tended to in preparation for deliveries. The din of a

767's engines being run up for the first time echoes across the airport. Parked near the centre is a British Airways 747-400 to be delivered in several weeks. Further down the line is a Cathay Pacific 777-300. It was the first of the stretched 777 models to enter service after its delivery in May 1998, once the test programme was complete. A 747-400 and 777, both in the colours of Saudi Arabian Airlines, and a United Airlines 777 also await their delivery day. A Boeing fire truck is parked at one stand as a precaution as a China Airlines 747-400 is fuelled for the first time.

On average, Boeing delivers about 15 wide-bodies a month, three or four a week, from Everett. Boeing's narrow-body 757s and 737s are built at Renton, near Seattle, and delivered from Boeing Field in the city's south end.

The Everett delivery centre has several large boardrooms where airline officials meet with Boeing staff to complete the paperwork on multi-million dollar deals in preparation to fly away the jet they had ordered in some cases years before. In one room, a team from Delta Air Lines is taking possession of a 767. Staff from British Airways have set up shop in another boardroom to work on the 777 delivery.

The minor headache of the FBW battery has been solved, only to be replaced with another snag, this time of a bureaucratic nature involving an avionics unit called a multi-mode receiver. This piece of equipment incorporates the ILS, microwave landing system (MLS)

and GPS functions into one integrated unit. More and more airports are getting instrument approaches based on GPS. As a result, airlines will soon be operating into airports with different landing systems, requiring aircraft to have the capability to fly more than one type of landing system. The multi-mode receiver allows an aircraft not only to fly ILS approaches now in use but to utilise GPS approaches as they come on line as well as MLS approaches. 'India Kilo' is the first 777 to be delivered with a multi-mode receiver and there is a slight delay as regulatory authorities work out the certification issues surrounding this equipment.

Considering that British Airways staff based at the factory and their counterparts at Boeing have devoted the last few weeks preparing for this day, the actual delivery is a surprisingly low-key event. Earlier in the day, the airline transferred money to a Boeing account to pay for the aircraft. Mid-afternoon, a handful of Boeing and British Airways staff gather in the boardroom and exchange signatures on a collection of documents to formalise the transaction. Barely an hour later, the airline has taken possession of a shiny new 777-236IGW — and

gets a receipt for its purchase. By this time, Chris and Kevin have set to work planning the 4,266nm flight to Heathrow.

Earlier in the day, a representative of the Federal Aviation Administration, the United States regulatory authority, examined the aircraft and, finding that it was built in conformity with the type certificate, issued the paperwork required to export the jet. The jet was also examined the previous day by an inspector from the Civil Aviation Authority, Britain's counterpart to the FAA. Once the sale is complete, the CAA issues a certificate of registration and a certificate of airworthiness.

At 6.15pm, British Airways' newest addition to the fleet is ready for departure. A small crowd of Boeing and British Airways staff has gathered at the edge of the

Below:
Captain Chris Parsons makes a radio selection as the end of the ocean crossing draws near.

taxiway to see the flight off. While such events are routine at Everett, there remains something special about the delivery of a new jet.

Accompanying the two pilots are three passengers who certainly have their choice of seats in the empty cabin. In a sense, this is the jet's first revenue flight because it is carrying some 30 tonnes of cargo. Cleared for take-off, the 777 accelerates along Runway 34 Left and takes to the air where it is swallowed up by the low overcast. Nineteen minutes and 148nm after take-off, the flight levels at 37,000ft. It is another 4,118nm to London. The 8hr 22min flight will be the longest yet for the new jet. Until now, it has logged 14hr and 32min in four flights, including its first flight which lasted 2hr 15min.

The routeing takes the 777 over the Canadian provinces of Alberta, Saskatchewan and Manitoba, across the expanse of Hudson Bay to 62° North and 50° West. From there it follows the 62nd parallel over the southern part of Greenland. The jet flies well north of the organised oceanic track system where most of the eastbound commercial flights are flying. After nearly 7hr in darkness, the sun rises on the nose, ending a long night sustained by many cups of tea. The jet passes over Belfast and the Isle of Man. Approach control brings the 777 over London to intercept the final approach for

Above:
Dawn brings an end to the long night and sunlight floods the flightdeck. London is just an hour away.

Runway 27 Right at Heathrow under a cloudless sky. Kevin eases the aircraft onto the runway with a gentle touch. They taxi across the airport to the British Airways cargo facility on the south side. The door is swung open and a crowd of maintenance staff comes aboard. Two other airline employees clamber up the airstairs and into the cabin laden with rolls of toilet paper. It is their job to stock the aircraft with everything needed for revenue service: in-flight magazines, fluffy pillows, blankets, boxes of facial tissue, soap, aftershave, colognes, hand towels and, of course, airsickness bags.

Within days, the jet will join the airline's 15 other 777s on revenue routes, the start of its 20 to 25-year life as a commercial jetliner, flying an average of 12hr a day. As shall be seen in the following chapters, the fleet is kept busy. Each day brings a new destination for British Airways' 777s.

Pre-Flight

The bus eases to a stop at the side of the road and the door swings open to admit the group of people standing at the kerbside. They climb aboard, take a seat and the bus pulls away for the next stop a short distance up the road. As it goes along its appointed route the bus is little different from the many others out shuttling morning commuters around the London area.

The topics of conversation among the passengers are typical for people riding into work — politics, the morning headlines and friendly banter.

But for these 'commuters' this short bus ride is only the start of their day's travels. By the time their workday is done, they will have spanned thousands of miles and will likely be spending the night in a hotel room far from home in destinations as varied as Antigua, Dallas and Rio de Janeiro.

They are all pilots and cabin staff with British Airways, riding on one of the company shuttle buses that run between the car parks and the crew reporting centre at London's Gatwick Airport.

The bus eases to a stop outside the centre and the crews disembark and make their way into the building, bags in tow. Among them is Captain Kevin Mottram, a 27-year veteran with the airline. On this February day, he will be in charge of British Airways Flight 2227 from Gatwick to Atlanta's Hartsfield International Airport on a Boeing 777.

Until this week, all of the airline's 777 flights had been out of Heathrow. But in one sign of Gatwick's evolution as a major hub for the airline, 777 service had been launched at the airport just a few days earlier with a flight to Bermuda, replacing a DC-10 on the three-times-a-week service. Kevin's flight today is the inaugural 777 run to Atlanta which will replace the daily DC-10 service that British Airways has operated since inheriting the route from British Caledonian many years earlier.

The flight is scheduled to depart at 10.55am London time which also happens to be the same in Co-ordinated Universal Time (UTC) and arrive at 20.30 UTC or 3.30pm Eastern Standard Time, Atlanta's time zone. To eliminate confusion, the aviation world operates on one time, known as UTC; all time references in the book will be UTC.

With the 777 operation new to Gatwick, it has been a while since Kevin last flew from the airport and he has arrived early to give himself plenty of time to find his way around.

The reporting centre is housed in a tired old building on the airport's south side and at this time of day it is bustling as dozens of pilots and flight attendants check in for morning flights. Kevin's first stop is the luggage drop-off on the main floor where he leaves his suitcase, then it is upstairs to the pilots' briefing room. The room overlooks the threshold of Runway 26 Left where an ATR-72 turboprop, Boeing 737, a Monarch DC-10 all await their turn for departure. The windows rattle from the roar of a departing British Airways 737-200.

Kevin goes to one of a cluster of computer terminals in the centre of the room and signs on. Here he checks on-line maintenance snags for the aircraft and finds there are no significant mechanical problems. Obviously, any serious problems are rectified before the next flight but some minor defects can be carried over for a few flights before repair. The Minimum Equipment List spells out exactly what equipment is required for flight and what gear can be flown unserviceable.

Using the computer he can also check details of the passenger load and Kevin learns there will be two infants, one unaccompanied minor, five VIPs and one wheelchair passenger among those travelling to Atlanta today.

With that task done, there is time for Kevin to nip down to the ground floor cafeteria for a quick bite of breakfast. There he meets a DC-10 captain familiar with Atlanta who is able to pass on some intelligence about the operations there. He says the US controllers prefer flights to accept a visual approach, which allows for closer spacing, and he says holds are common. More importantly, he draws Kevin a map showing the best restaurants around the crew hotel!

Right:
The pilots of British Airways Flight 2227 meet in the briefing room to review the paperwork for their flight to Atlanta — Captain Kevin Mottram, left, and Senior First Officer Graeme Lunn, middle, are joined by First Officer Rehman Shivjee, who will act as relief pilot on the journey.

```
P 1 OF 9 BA2227/6 LGW-ATL ETD  1055/06FEB98 777/2 G-VIIJ
        ETOPS ETPS CRITICAL FUEL/TIME VALIDATED 180 MINS
C/S BAW7N    M 0.0 EGKK-KATL M 5.0  T/O SLOT ....

183.3 --ZFW-- .... 2030 ATA .... TNKS ....    3 MNTH ROUTE STATS

250.9   TOW   .... 1055 ATD .... USED ....    NO DATA AVAILABLE

192.5   LAW   .... 0935 TOT .... LEFT ....

 36.5   PL    .... HOLD W A .... ACH FL ....

TRIM .....   MIN COST - FP  NO. 2  0822 06FEB98

ROUTE 02AS -  FL350  5510N/FL370  FOXXE/FL390
NAT TRK F
TIF .......   58413  8.51  3855NM W/C M38          TOC DAT M57
CONT ......    1748    19  ERA JFK /KJFK          WIND  25035
DIVC ......    4800    39  CLT /KCLT FL170 P8 227NM
RES .......    2659    30  PLAN REM 9.2 TOT RES 7.5
RED .......   67620 10.19                   COST INDEX   100
EXTRA ......      0        WX ATC ......
TAXI .......    640   (20)
TANKS ......  68260 KG                           ELEV ATL 1026
SIX EIGHT TWO SIX ZERO  KG

OHDIV ......   1968    34  CLT /KCLT FROM FL410 P14 227NM
DIV2 ......    6848  1.01  MCO /KMCO FL370 M8 392NM

WEIGHT CHANGE P 5000 KG  FP 1251 KG  TM 1  TRIP FUEL
FL350  5510N/FL360  FOXXE/FL390  MOL/FL350
HEIGHT CHANGE M *** NOT CALCULATED ***
SPEED  CHANGE CI   0      FP 98 KG  TP 1  TRIP FUEL
FL350  5510N/FL360  FOXXE/FL390

RMKS ETOPS 180MIN RULE PLAN...   RTOW 26L MAX
  **NBT E SAME TIME/FUEL**
    ETOPS ERA EGCC CYYR
```

Shortly after 09.00Z, Kevin returns to the briefing room where he meets up with Senior First Officer Graeme Lunn. First Officer Rehman Shivjee has also been assigned to augment the crew as a relief pilot to spell off the other two pilots during cruise. The rules are complex but generally a relief pilot is required whenever the chock-to-chock time exceeds 9hr.

The aircraft they are flying today is the 777-236IGW. Although the flight to Atlanta will be the longest of those flown by the airline's 777s, it is well within the jet's maximum range.

The three pilots exchange introductions and gather at the briefing counter where the documents, weather maps and flightplan are spread out for easy examination. Details of the flightplan have been prepared by staff at the airline's operations centre at Heathrow. There, dispatchers on the Atlantic desk have done flightplans for the 40 British Airways flights that will cross the ocean this day, including one planner dedicated to the specialised planning required for the 11 transatlantic flights by 777s, 767s and 757s. Operating a twin-engined jet on such long over-water legs is a special type of flying. It is known as extended-range, twin-engine operations (ETOPS) and it refers to the portion of the flight more than 60min away from an airport if the aircraft has to divert with one engine shut down. Most twin commercial jets have regulatory approval to fly 180min from an airport, meaning there is little restriction on North Atlantic routes. Still, flight planners must ensure the weather at airports like Shannon, Gander and Goose Bay makes them acceptable as en route alternates.

The flightplan for BA 2227 stretches to nine pages of computer print-out, all of it a treasure trove of information about the journey. It lays out the optimum routeing for the flight, accounting for such factors as significant weather, airspace restrictions and most importantly, the winds aloft. It tells the pilots the distance between each of the 38 en route waypoints, the time it will take to fly each leg, the minimum fuel required at the end of each leg and even the minimum safe altitude for each part of the route.

From Gatwick, the jet will head west to a waypoint just west of Southampton called GIBSO to pick up the airway UR14. Airways are like highways in the sky that connect radio beacons. From there it will track UR14 northwest across the Bristol Channel to the Strumble VOR radio beacon in Wales, then across the Irish Sea to Dublin. There, it will follow airway UN560 direct to 55° North latitude and 10° West longitude (shortened to 5510N) for the start of the ocean crossing.

The airspace over the North Atlantic is unique and is not organised on the usual system of airways. Instead, to ensure safety and organise flow, aircraft crossing the ocean fly along designated routes called the Oceanic Track System developed by the two air traffic control centres responsible for the bulk of the traffic over the Atlantic.

Noise curfews, time differences and airport curfews mean there are two peak flows to the North Atlantic traffic — eastbound from North America during the night and early morning and westbound from Europe in the late morning and afternoon. To accommodate these flows, the tracks are revised twice every 24hr, once for each direction, and take into account the weather conditions to allow as many aircraft as possible to fly the most economical routeings. Daytime tracks are selected by air traffic controllers in Prestwick, Scotland, who plot the routeings so westbound flights can avoid the worst of the prevailing headwinds. Likewise, the eastbound tracks are plotted by controllers in Gander, Newfoundland, to take advantage of the best tailwinds.

These parallel transoceanic highways are laid out one degree of latitude, or 60nm, apart and labelled for easy identification. Westbound tracks are Alpha, Bravo, Charlie, Delta, Echo and Foxtrot. Tracks in the opposite direction are Uniform, Victor, Whiskey, X-ray, Yankee and Zulu.

Aircraft flying the North Atlantic are beyond radar coverage for most of the route, making it imperative they navigate accurately to avoid conflicts. The oceanic tracks are within what is called minimum navigation performance specification airspace. This requires aircraft to have two operating inertial navigational units for redundancy and minimise any chance of a navigational error.

Today's tracks have been laid out well to the north to avoid a strong jetstream that is blowing across the mid-North Atlantic in excess of 150kt at 33,000ft. A headwind of this strength would add up to an hour to an ocean crossing. Avoiding it saves time and fuel.

The crew note that the dispatcher has selected Track Foxtrot, the southernmost of six tracks. This will take the flight over 5720N, 5930N, 5940N, 5750N to LOACH, a waypoint just off Canada's Labrador coast, and then into Canadian domestic airspace.

The co-ordinates for Track Foxtrot on the flightplan are compared against a separate print-out of the day's Atlantic tracks to ensure the two match. This is just one of the many checks in place to guard against navigational mix-ups. An error in just one co-ordinate could send the plane across an adjacent track, creating a conflict.

The flight will continue across Labrador, over the St Lawrence River to Albany in upper New York State, then west of Washington, DC and down to Atlanta. The Boeing 777 is expected to cover the 3,855nm trip in 8hr 51min, cruising at Mach 0.84. Knots are not used as a prime speed reference at higher altitudes because of errors caused by low air density. Instead, speed is measured as a percentage of the speed of sound, or Mach number. For example, the 777's typical cruise speed of Mach 0.84 is 84% of the speed of sound.

Below:
The significant weather chart for the North Atlantic shows a strong jetstream blowing across the middle of the ocean.

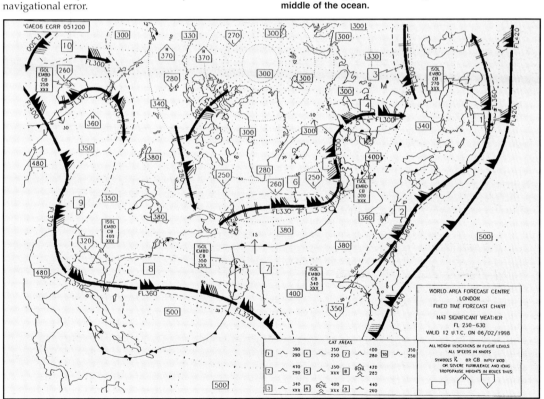

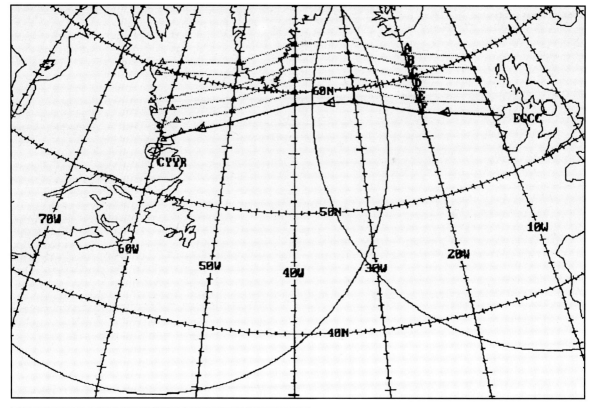

```
ATLANTA HARTSFIELD
ATL   SA060900   0608532 30012KT 10SM OVC015 01/M02 A2982 RMK AO2
KATL             SLP107
      SA060800   0607532 31008KT 10SM OVC015 01/M02 A2982 RMK AO2
                 SLP106
      FT060535   0608202 060606 32012G22KT P6SM OVC018 TEMPO 0610
                 OVC022 FM1000 31010KT P6SM OVC015 TEMPO 1014 OVC022
                 FM1400 30008KT P6SM OVC025 TEMPO 1523 BKN035 -

KATL ---RWY 09L ILS LLZ U/S 25 DEG RIGHT OF RWY CL.
ATL  ---INBND CREWS TO CALL DELTA RAMP 129.37
     ///WEF 06 FEB ALL DEPS WILL OPR UNDER CLC PROC. PROVISIONAL
        LOADSHEETS WITH NAME/LICENCE NBR OF THE LOAD CONTROLLER
        WILL BE PRODUCED BY THE CLC CENTER IN IAD. FINAL LOADSHEET
        DETAILS WILL BE PASSED VIA ACARS. ATL COY VHF TO BE USED AS
        FALLBACK IN THE CASE OF ACARS FAILURE.

************   SWORD ALTERNATES FOR ATL   ***********************

CHARLOTTE DOUGLAS
CLT   SA060900   0608502 34004KT 10SM BKN040 OVC055 06/01 A2978 RMK
KCLT  SA060800   0607502 34005KT 10SM SCT037 OVC055 06/01 A2978 RMK
      FT060540   0608382 060606 VRB03KT P6SM OVC040 TEMPO 0609 OVC030
                 FM0900 VRB03KT P6SM OVC035 TEMPO 0913 OVC025 FM1300
                 02005KT P6SM BKN035 BECMG 1416 SCT035 BKN250 FM2100
                 02006KT P6SM SCT040 BKN250 BECMG 0002 OVC040 -
```

Top:
Today's oceanic routes have been laid out well to the north to avoid the strong headwinds. British Airways Flight 2227 has requested Track Foxtrot, the southernmost track.

Above:
A print-out showing the current and forecast weather conditions for Atlanta along with the Notices to Airmen (NOTAMS) which alert pilots to anything which could affect operations at the airport. Also included is the weather for Charlotte, North Carolina, the diversionary landing airport.

The flightplan suggests cruising at 37,000ft initially, then climbing to 39,000ft after the ocean crossing when a good portion of the fuel has been burned off and the jet is tonnes lighter.

The dispatcher's calculations show the flight will require 68.3 tonnes of fuel: 58.4 tonnes for the trip itself; 1.8 tonnes of contingency fuel; 4.8 tonnes of diversion fuel should it have to fly to Charlotte, North Carolina, the designated landing alternate airport; and a further 2.7 tonnes of reserve fuel which is enough to fly for 30min at the predicted landing weight. Another 640kg of fuel is planned for start-up and taxi at Gatwick.

The crew have the final authority and can request extra fuel if they expect delays due to weather or air traffic control. But the flightplans are generally very accurate and crews must balance adding 'a little extra for mother' against the cost of tankering unnecessary fuel. Fuel weighs 7lb per US gal and every extra gallon can mean less cargo or fewer passengers which eats into an airline's bottom line.

In a telling testament to the 777's twin-engine economics, a DC-10 would require 93 tonnes of fuel — a third more than the 777 — to fly the same route with the same payload and it would take 6min longer.

A separate package contains actual weather reports and forecasts for Gatwick, Atlanta and airports en route. Atlanta is expected to have an overcast ceiling of 2,500ft but otherwise good weather. The crew also pay close attention to conditions at Manchester and Goose Bay, the airfields selected as the ETOPS second-choice airports should a diversion be necessary over the ocean. The forecast for Manchester reveals good weather that will give way to a 3,500ft ceiling in rain showers. Goose is

```
FF EGKKBAWD
060822 EGLLBAWD
COMPANY ADDRESSEES
(FPL-BAW7N-IS
-B777/H-SXRW/C
-EGKK1055
-N0478F350 DCT SAM UR8 GIBSO UR14 DUB UN560 ERNAN UN550
 55N010W/M084F370 NATF FOXXE/N0489F390 N272B
-KATL0846 KCLT
-EET/EISN0038 EGPX0057 EGGX0107 CZQX0242 CZQM0449 FOXXE0503
 CZUL0530 KZBW0641 KZNY0714 KZDC0737 KZTL0805
 REG/GVIIJ SEL/GKFR
 RMK/ETOPS ERA EGCC CYYR AGCS EQUIPPED TCAS EQUIPPED)
```

forecasting a layer of broken cloud at 2,500ft and more than six miles visibility in light snow showers. The temperature there is a chilly -19° Celsius. In both cases, the weather is well above the minimums required for diversions.

The significant weather chart shows no serious weather en route, apart from the possibility early in the flight of some clear air turbulence around 35,000ft when the flight crosses the jetstream northwest of Ireland.

Finally, the crew pore over the Notices to Airmen (NOTAMS). These are alerts about construction work, unserviceable radio beacons and other such items that could impact on the operation of a flight. The lengthy notes for Gatwick include details about a closed taxiway, a new ATC frequency and a note urging pilots not to land before 6am local time when a night jet ban is in effect, even if it means delaying a departure from another city or reducing speed en route.

The paperwork is collected and the crew prepare to head out to the aircraft. Kevin takes a minute to pop into a meeting room where the cabin staff have gathered for their own briefing, led by Cabin Service Director Mark Howden who will oversee cabin operations on the flight. Because the Boeing 777 is new to the Gatwick-based crews, the flight attendants devote some extra time to reviewing emergency procedures and the location of emergency equipment throughout the cabin.

When the cabin crew and pilots have completed their duties at the reporting centre, they make their way downstairs. Not even airline staff are spared the pre-boarding security checks. However, the crew go through security and have their luggage X-rayed at the reporting centre, bypassing the crowds and queues in the terminal. At 09.45Z the crew board the bus for the short ride to the aircraft parked at Gate 52 at the North Terminal.

The 777 assigned to the Atlanta flight is G-VIIJ, or 'India Juliet', which has been in service with British Airways for just over a month after its delivery in late December 1997. Yesterday, it flew back to Heathrow from Dhahran and then was ferried to Gatwick for today's flight.

'India Juliet' is painted in the bold new livery unveiled by British Airways in 1997, its tenth anniversary as a privatised airline. A brighter colour scheme has replaced the traditional red, grey and midnight blue design. A wavy three-dimensional 'speedmarque' on the nose is used in place of the red speedwing along the fuselage and the name 'British Airways' appears in softer, rounder typeface.

The biggest change though is on the tails of the aircraft in the fleet. For its tail art, British Airways is using 50 different world images, drawn from artists around the globe. The tail of 'India Juliet' features the image 'Benyhome', a Scottish highland tartan design called Mountain of Birds created by weaver Peter MacDonald. Other designs include a work from the Bushmen of the Kalahari, Celtic calligraphy, a painted wood carving from Canada's northwest and the work of a graffiti artist from Amsterdam. Understandably, the new livery was introduced with some controversy. Some critics bemoan the lack of anything 'British' or a common theme to the tail art. Yet even those not enamoured with the designs do admit they are distinctive.

Many of the aircraft parked at the North Terminal are British Airways jets, a sign of the airline's growing presence at Gatwick.

The North Terminal celebrated its 10th anniversary in March 1998, and its traffic figures since opening are a good indication of how Gatwick has become a major international airport. In its first 12 months of operation, the terminal handled 4.7 million passengers with an average of 98 flights a day. Ten years later, the facility was handling more than 12 million travellers annually and averaging 283 daily flights. Overall, in 1997 the airport itself saw 26.9 million passengers, up 10.8% from 1996, and 441,449 flights — an impressive total considering Gatwick is a one-runway operation.

Above:
A copy of the flightplan filed with air traffic control.

Below:
G-VIIJ, a Boeing 777-236IGW, is the centre of activity at Gate 52 at Gatwick's North Terminal as it is readied for the transatlantic trip.

With the runway capacity at Heathrow airport becoming constrained, British Airways is rapidly developing Gatwick as its second major London hub. By 1997, British Airways and its partner airlines served more destinations from Gatwick than Heathrow, thanks to a combination of growth and a transfer of routes from Heathrow. The move began in earnest in 1996 when British Airways launched 71 new routes from Gatwick. Now the airline and its partners serve more than 100 destinations from Gatwick and in 1997 launched new services linking the airport to Glasgow, Barcelona, Lisbon and St Petersburg. The airline also transferred its Latin America services to Gatwick, adding to the east and central Africa flights it had moved earlier. Several of the new 777s are based at Gatwick to handle the growth. By 1999, the mix of aircraft types used on intercontinental services from Gatwick will be rationalised into three types — 747-400s, 777s and 767-300ERs. The airline — which already handles one-quarter of all passengers at Gatwick — expects its passenger traffic at the airport to double by 2003.

British Airways' traditional red, grey and midnight blue paint scheme has been replaced by a brighter colour scheme as shown in these two photos. A distinctive change is the tail art which features one of 50 world images.
British Airways (above)/John M. Dibbs (top)

As the crew head to the jet, passengers have also begun to congregate in the departure lounge and can watch the pre-flight preparations from the bay windows that overlook the ramp. The aircraft is a hub of activity. It is the pilots, flight attendants and passenger agents that a passenger sees during a trip but a virtual army is at work behind the scenes to ensure the safe and efficient operation of each flight. British Airways employs more than 58,000 people — just more than 200 employees for each of the 256 aircraft in its fleet. Preparations for this flight actually started months earlier when the airline's planners decided what type of aircraft would be used on what routes for the winter schedule, the marketing department set the fares and crews were assigned to the flight. Now, on the day of the departure, dispatchers have planned the route, meals have been prepared in the flight kitchens, ramp staff are at work loading cargo into the jet and maintenance staff are doing their last-minute checks. Considering that British Airways repeats this exercise for each of its 1,000 daily departures, one gets a sense of the huge logistical effort required to keep a large airline running smoothly — and on time.

The three flight crew members enter the flightdeck through a door in front of the first class galley just behind the captain's seat. The flight bags are stowed where they can be easily reached during flight. Because of the importance of pilot comfort on long-haul trips, Boeing paid careful attention to the layout and features of the flightdeck, right down to the improved storage for bulky flightbags and carry-on luggage.

There is plenty of work yet to be done. Kevin has elected to be the handling pilot and Graeme will look after the radios and flight logs. It is also the job of the non-handling pilot to monitor the actions of the pilot doing the flying, make the standard call-outs and draw attention to any deviations from the desired altitude, speed, heading or attitude.

The world of the airline pilot is based on well-versed actions that come as a result of training and procedures. Everything from the walk-around to the take-off and landing is done in a standard fashion, with a checklist for each phase of the flight to ensure nothing is missed. Two pilots may be flying together for the first time but thanks to this well-honed routine, they know exactly what to expect from each other at every point in the flight.

In that vein, there are specific jobs spelled out for the handling pilot and non-handling pilot in this time leading up to departure and Kevin's first task is to carry out the exterior inspection.

He dons a safety vest, exits the aircraft and descends a staircase from the jetway to the ramp. London has been enjoying a spell of unseasonably warm, dry weather and today is another nice day which makes it a pleasure to do the walk-around. It is quite another thing to do it with flashlight in hand on a cold night in lashing rain.

Maintenance staff have already done their own walk-around of the aircraft as part of a check required of all ETOPS flights. However, since final responsibility for the flight rests with the pilots, they perform their own checks.

During the walk-around Kevin is examining the general condition of the jet, looking for things like dents in the aircraft skin, leaks of oil, hydraulic fluid or fuel, and making sure doors and access panels are closed. Starting at the front of the aircraft, he examines the nose gear and checks that the pitot tubes and static ports on both sides of the nose are uncovered. Also on each side of the nose are ice detector probes. When either probe senses ice and the flightdeck anti-ice switches are set to AUTO, engine anti-ice valves automatically open. Hot bleed air from the engine is piped in to heat the engine inlet cowls and prevent the formation of ice. If the probes detect ice several times, the leading edges of each wing are de-iced by the hot air as well.

Kevin continues the walk-around along the right wing, looking at the landing lights, right engine and strut and the tarmac under the engine to ensure there is no fluid dripping. He examines the wing itself, the leading edge slats, aileron, flap and flaperon. Moving back under the fuselage, he checks the huge main gear, paying close attention to brake lines and the condition of the tyres, looking for cuts, scuff marks, bulges or uneven

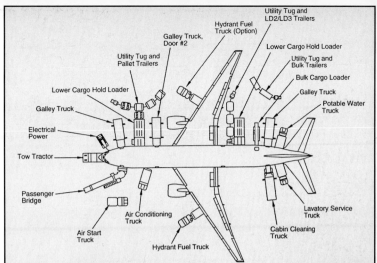

Top:
A typical arrangement for servicing the 777 at the gate.
Boeing

Middle
Fresh from the flight kitchen: the food and beverage carts are wheeled onboard from the catering truck.

Above:
Three hats hanging on the flightdeck bulkhead indicate a relief pilot is part of the flight crew and suggest the trip is a long one.

Above:
As the handling pilot, Kevin is responsible for the exterior inspection of the aircraft. He begins at the front of the jet with a close look at the nose gear.

Above right:
The inspection continues around the trailing edge of the right wing...

Right:
...the unique six-wheeled main gear...

Below right:
....and the left engine. At 123in, the diameter of the fan on the massive GE90 is about equal to the fuselage of the Boeing 727.

wear on the rubber. Looking up in the wheel well, he checks that the downlock pins, which prevent the wheels from being retracted, have not been inserted. Though these pins are used only during maintenance on the landing gear, this simple check avoids getting airborne only to find the gear will not retract! He walks under the tail, looking at the horizontal stabiliser, the rudder and the vertical stabiliser which towers more than 60ft above him. He moves up the left side of the aircraft, around the left wing and engine and returns to the nose.

Parked under the left wing is a fuel truck which is pumping fuel from a hydrant located in the tarmac up into a fuelling port in the wing's leading edge just outboard of the engine. The IGW model has two wing tanks, each with a capacity of 9,560gal, and a large centre tank that can hold 26,100gal of fuel — 13,700gal more than the base model which gives the IGW model its long legs. The underwing fuelling station has a panel that allows the fueller to set the total required fuel load. Refuel valves automatically open to fill the wing tanks first and then the centre tank until the desired amount is reached. The flight arrived with 7.6 tonnes of fuel and the truck is pumping another 60.7 tonnes of jet fuel — about 19,000 US gal — into the aircraft.

Up on the flightdeck, Graeme is well into his own preparations for the flight. He first confirms that the APU is running. This is a small jet engine located in the tail section which supplies electrical power and compressed air to aircraft systems, giving some measure of independence when the main engines are shut down. The compressed air is passed through the air conditioning system to heat or cool the cabin prior to start-up. Once the engines are running, engine bleed air takes over the job. Air from the APU is also used to spin the engines for start.

He then does a security inspection to ensure no suspicious package has been hidden on the flightdeck and checks that emergency equipment such as fire gloves, smoke hoods, life jackets, escape ropes and fire extinguisher are all in place.

He surveys the aircraft library to ensure the required titles are onboard, stowed in the many cupboards around the flightdeck. The titles are varied but include the minimum equipment list, 777 technical manual and performance manual, flight documents folder, en route maps and emergency airfields manual.

With those checks complete, Graeme can settle into the right seat to begin the scan check, a detailed examination of the flightdeck instrumentation to ensure switches and systems are properly configured for start-up. It begins on the overhead panel, continues across the glareshield and the autoflight controls, the instrument panel and standby instruments, then down the centre console. The check runs to several pages in the 777 flying manual and includes such actions as ensuring engine autostart is ON, fuel pumps are OFF and cabin and flightdeck temperature controls are set. Across the glareshield, the autothrottle is armed and flight directors are turned ON and electronic checklists are reset. On the centre console, the parking brake is checked set, speedbrake lever down, thrust levers closed and fuel control switches in the CUTOFF position and the emergency evacuation alarm is tested.

As well, the window heat is selected ON to prevent frosting inflight and provide resiliency against a birdstrike. Wing and engine anti-ice selectors are set to AUTO.

Vital take-off data such as V-speeds, engine derate and flap setting are obtained via the datalink. Graeme uses the CDU to enter information such as the airport, runway in use and whether it is wet or dry, temperature, barometric pressure and the estimated take-off weight. The data is then transmitted to a computer at Heathrow which runs an electronic version of the aircraft flight manual in conjunction with an airfield database. Within minutes a piece of paper with the desired information appears from the printer in the centre console.

Rehman, sitting in one of the two jumpseats, has tuned Gatwick's automatic terminal information service (ATIS). This taped broadcast provides weather conditions, runway in use and other airfield information and is updated at least once an hour or more often when weather conditions are changing fast.

Gatwick ATIS: 'This is Gatwick information Whiskey. The one zero one five hours weather, runway in use is two-six left, wind is two one zero degrees at seven knots, variable between one eight zero and two four zero degrees. Visibility is 25 kilometres, nil weather. Cloud, few at 2,500 feet. Air temperature is plus nine, dewpoint plus five. QNH is one zero two one millibars, QFE is one zero one four millibars. On first contact with Gatwick report information Whiskey received.'

At 10.20Z, the Captain arrives back on the flightdeck. He first does his own scan check along the sidewall and the controls for his PFD and ND. He then refers to the aircraft's technical log for any outstanding deficiencies logged by the last crew. Finding no squawks, he sets to work on the important task of preparing the FMC for the flight. Using the CDU, he first enters the jet's current position into the FMC, using the latitude and longitude given by the GPS. This provides the computer with a starting reference point for navigation purposes.

Below:
Back on board the aircraft, Kevin reviews the aircraft technical manual to see what snags were logged by previous crews and the corrective action taken by maintenance staff.

Above:
Kevin loads the FMC with details of the flight. This once time-consuming process has been made easier by the ability to download the routeing and winds directly into the jet's computer via datalink.

Above:
Kevin loads the FMC with details of the flight. This once time-consuming process has been made easier by the ability to download the routeing and winds directly into the jet's computer via datalink.

Opposite above:
Flying a twin-engined jet across the ocean requires special planning considerations. This 777 ETOPS and Atlantic planning guide highlights some of the items considered by pilots during such a flight. *British Airways*

Opposite below:
Performance data for take-off is obtained via the datalink.

He then uses the datalink to download details of the flightplan from the central airline computer into the FMC. What he gets back is an electronic version of the flightplan that stretches to nine pages of paper. To complete the process, he pushes the buttons activate and execute. Within just minutes, Kevin has loaded the jet's computer with the routeing to Atlanta.

These few keystrokes replace the hundreds previously required to load a flight of this length manually into the FMC. Using the datalink is not only a tremendous labour-saving device, it also eliminates the possibility of mistyping a waypoint into the computer, a simple mistake that has caused several cases of gross navigation errors, sometimes with potentially dangerous conflicts with aircraft flying on adjacent oceanic tracks.

Selecting from a menu on the CDU, Kevin enters the departure runway and standard instrument departure (SID) likely to be flown today. With the SID selected, the FMC automatically tunes and identifies the required radio beacons and displays the departure routeing on the ND.

Both pilots verify details of the programmed route by cross-checking waypoints and distances against those on the printed plan and the route that has been filed with ATC. Kevin sends two more datalink messages to load the FMC with the winds en route and the diversionary airports.

The aircraft dispatcher has brought the crew the provisional loadsheet. This dispatcher — different from the one who did the flightplan — co-ordinates cargo loading, cleaning of the cabin, fuelling, passenger enplaning and the many other activities needed to get the aircraft away on time.

According to the preliminary weight figures, the jet has been loaded with 24,616kg of cargo and baggage in its belly. The 164 passengers and their carry-on bags add another 13,448kg for a total payload of 38,064kg. This is added to the jet's dry operating weight of 146,748kg for a zero fuel weight of 184,812kg. The amount of food and beverages required for more than 150 people on a 9hr flight is not insignificant — the aircraft is loaded with 5 tonnes of catering and duty-free items. With just over 68 tonnes of fuel onboard, take-off weight will be 252,472kg. That is well under the maximum take-off weight of 267,619kg.

With this weight and balance information available, Kevin turns his attention to the take-off performance data. He confirms the fuel load — 28.9 tonnes in the left

777 ETOPS and ATLANTIC PLANNING GUIDE

ERA DECODES

BGSF	SFJ	Sondrestrom
BIKF	KEF	Keflavik
CYFB	YFB	Iqaluit (Frobisher)
CYHZ	YHZ	Halifax
CYQX	YQX	Gander
CYYR	YYR	Goose
CYYT	YYT	St. Johns (Torbay)
LPAZ	SMA	Santa Maria
LPLA	TER	Lajes

Pre-Flight Requirements

In addition to normal documents -
* Flight Progress Chart / EROPA
* NAT Track Signal

AIS, MET and Planning

* Valid to STD + 1hour
* Departure airfield, return alternate.
* Destination & alternate (ref USA alternate minima in Performance Manual).
* ERAs 'suitable' - at or above planning minima during time window.
* Forecasts: PROB less than 40% ignored. Few and scattered ignored.
* Minima can be reduced by 200ft/ 700m for 2 suitable runways / airfields.

SWORD

* ETOPS valid.
* ERAs as EROPA.
* Critical Fuel.
* ETPs.

ATC Flight Plan

* X-check with SWORD & NAT signal.

EROPA & Flight Progress Chart

* Correct rule distance.
* Correct route, date and ERAs.

Verification flights.

* ETOPs and Non ETOPs
* Swords & fuel for both.
* ETOPs ATC may be filed.
* Check landing weight.

At the Aircraft

* Check Tech Log ADDs, verification requirements
* ETOPS PDC signature
* When Flight Plan route has been executed, select Hdg Ref to True and check SWORD Initial True Tracks (ITT) and distances against FMC.

Clearances

* Confirmed by both pilots and resolve doubts.

Prior to MNPS Entry

* Obtain Oceanic clearance (see reverse of Flight Progress Chart).
* If cleared route different from planned, modify Route in FMC and check FMC Initial True Tracks (ITT) and distances against track signal.

Entering MNPS

* Check NAV accuracy (FMC, ADIRU, GPS, Radio indications on ND).
* Set cleared Mach Number in FMC.
* Set Hdg Ref to True.
* Squawk A2000 after 30min.
* Monitor 121.5 and 131.8.

Crossing waypoints

* Check NAV accuracy (FMC, ADIRU, GPS indications on ND).
* Check ITT and distance to next waypoint.
* Check aircraft turns on to required track on ND.
* Make position report, copy position report to next OCA if at 10 deg before 30W and at 30W.
* Carry out fuel check.

General Awareness

* ETA for ETPs.
* FMC ALTN page gives howgozit to nearest ERAs.
* Weather at ERAs - normal minima now apply.
* Critical fuel at ETPs.
* Advise Maintrol of result of Verification.

Leaving MNPS

* Obtain domestic clearance.
* Return Hdg Ref to Norm.
* Select Econ cruise speed and request Optimum FL.

Post Flight Retain

* Flight Progress Chart with route flown shown.
* Nubrief - (relevant section)
* Wx reports ERAs Dest Alts
* Make tech log verification entry if appropriate.

Re-route procedure

* Confirm rule compliance from EROPA or Flight Progress Chart. Confirm compliance with Critical Fuel Scenario. Flight Crew Briefing can provide assistance.
* Check suitability of ERAs.
* Advise ATC new entry pt.
* RTE COPY?
* Modify FMC Route.
* Check ITT and distances from track signal or Route Information Manual.

Verification Flight Failure, Non ETOPS operation

* Advise Co of failure
* Arrival message

---

tank, 29 tonnes in the right and another 10.4 tonnes in the centre tank. This tank, rarely used on present British Airways routes, has a total capacity of 79 tonnes of fuel, giving some sense of the jet's unused range on today's flight.

Depending on aircraft weight and temperature, full power is not always required for take-off. Today is one of those days when graduated power is sufficient, saving engine wear and tear and extending engine life. The computer calculates the power required and then presents the pilots with an assumed temperature — today it is 36° Celsius — which is entered into the FMC. The system then works out the full power setting required for take-off at that temperature, resulting in less thrust on this cooler day.

Kevin enters the take-off flap setting — in this case, 15° — and 1,000ft as both the acceleration and thrust reduction altitude. At this height, the flight director will command a lower pitch attitude to accelerate for flap retraction and the engines will reduce thrust to climb power. The 777 enjoys good climb performance even at derated thrusts and heavy weights.

Next the crew review the important V-speeds for take-off: both V1, the decision speed, and VR, the rotation speed, are 148kt. V2, the single engine climb speed is 153kt.

V1 is the critical go or no-go decision speed. If a problem occurs before V1, sufficient runway is left to stop the aircraft safely. After V1, the jet is committed to take-off and the emergency will be handled once it is safely in the air. Most aircraft emergencies allow some

```
        PERFORMANCE DATA UPLINK MESSAGE

BA2227        06FEB98 10:26      G-VIIJ 85B
EGKK/26L      B1 HOLD            TORA 2884
W/C   2 TW    TEMP  9C           QNH 1022
DRY RWY       ANTI-ICE OFF       MACTOW  O

DAY : CLG NIL              VIS 150M
NIGHT: CLG NIL             VIS 150M
PVD 75M

PERF CORRS
NONE

FLAP 15   TOPL: 268.5

ATOW      TEMP     V1    VR    V2
258.6     34       149   150   156
255.0     36       149   149   155
250.3     38       148   148   153

NOTES
PERFORMANCE RESTRICTION

ENGINE FAILURE
TURN LEFT 15 DEG AT END OF RUNWAY.

2 OF 2
END OF MESSAGE
```

time to assess events and pilots are encouraged to think things out and avoid any rushed actions that could aggravate a problem. But an emergency on take-off is a very serious event, one of those few times a crew must act without delay. The engines are at full power, the aircraft is accelerating down the runway and pilots have only seconds to decide a safe course of action: continue or abort. For that reason, pilots are trained in simulator sessions to react instinctively to an emergency on take-off.

Above:
Graeme organises paperwork for the flight. As the non-handling pilot on this leg, he will look after the radios and the task of tracking times and fuel burns on the flight log.

Right:
Preparations are well under way in the cabin as flight attendants Yvette Brooks and Brian Devlin-Reid work in the forward galley.

Below right:
With their own specific tasks complete, the pilots come together for the departure briefing.

Opposite:
Chart showing the departure routeings from Gatwick. Today's flight will fly the Southampton Two Mike (SAM 2M) departure.
Racal Avionics

EGKK

T. Alt **6000**

G7

29 JAN 98

1. KENET SID restricted to traffic destination in UK or EIRE. 2. Initial climb: Ahead to 700. 3. On initial contact with London Control, include callsign, SID designator and current altitude/flight level. 4. En-route cruising level will be given by London Control after take-off. 5. Max 250kt below FL 100 unless otherwise authorised. 6. Cross noise monitoring points (see C1) not below 1200, thereafter min climb gradient of 4%(243'/nm) to 3000 for noise abatement requirements. 7. R/W 08L min gradient 5.5%(334'/nm) to 400 (R/W 26R min gradient not published).

G/S kt	100	130	160	190	220	250	
ft/min	410	530	650	770	890	1010	243'/nm
ft/min	560	720	890	1060	1230	1390	334'/nm

NOT TO SCALE

KENET
LON 37d
N51 31·2
W001 27·3

LON 277R

2 3 2 3
2 2 2 2
SSA 25nm

LON 113.6

SAM 2P,2W
KENET 2P,2W

DET 28d
2500 or above

DET 36d
at 3000

DET 43d
SAM 33d
at 4000

DET 117.3 263R

SAM 071R

331°

KENET 2M,2V

KENET 2P,2W

263°

'GY' 365
N51 07·8
W000 18·9
262°

4
I GG 3.5d
I GG/I WW
Ch 46
(110.9)

SAM 20d

14
251°

8
247°

MID 10d
above 2500

MID 8d
above 3000

SAM 2P,2W

49

20
251°

10
261°

18
261°

MID 10d

MIDHURST
MID 114.0
N51 03·2
W000 37.5

SOUTHAMPTON
SAM 113.35
N50 57·3
W001 20.7

SAM 2M,2V
KENET 2M,2V
at 4000

SAM 2M,2V

331R

25nm

Goodwood
GWC 114.75

WARNING
Due to interaction with other routes do NOT climb above specified intermediate altitudes unless cleared by ATC.

AVERAGE TRACK MILEAGE TO SAM	
SAM 2M,2V 44	
SAM 2P,2W 56	
TO KENET	
KENET 2M,2V 65	
KENET 2P,2W 71	

SID	R/W	ROUTEING(including Min Noise Routeing)	ALTITUDES
SAM 2M SAM 2V (134.125)	26L 26R	Ahead via GY maintaining Tr262M then left to intercept Tr247M(MID 067R) to MID. At MID right on MID 261R to SAM.	MID 10d above 2500 MID 8d above 3000 MID at 4000
SAM 2P SAM 2W (134.125)	08R 08L	Ahead to I GG 3.5d then left to intercept DET 263R. Left on Tr251M(SAM 071R) to SAM.	DET 28d 2500 or above DET 36d at 3000 DET 43d/SAM 33d at 4000
KENET 2M KENET 2V (134.125)	26L 26R	Ahead via GY maintaining Tr262M then left to intercept Tr247M(MID 067R) to MID. At MID right on MID 261R to MID 10d, then right on GWC 331R to KENET.	MID 10d above 2500 MID 8d above 3000 MID at 4000
KENET 2P KENET 2W (134.125)	08R 08L	Ahead to I GG 3.5d then left to intercept DET 263R. Left on Tr251M(SAM 071R). At SAM 20d right on GWC 331R to KENET.	DET 28d 2500 or above DET 36d at 3000 DET 43d/SAM 33d at 4000

Rev: Warning note.

WGS 84

41

The jet is equipped with an alert to help the pilots recognise and confirm an engine failure. On take-off, if an engine is not supplying the thrust commanded by the pilot or suffers a complete failure, an automated voice will call out 'Engine Fail', the master warning lights will illuminate and the message 'ENG FAIL' will appear on the PFDs.

Aborting a take-off is, for the most part, a decision made by the Captain. The First Officer is to call out any EICAS messages and the Captain will announce 'Stop' or 'Continue'. However, the First Officer can call 'Stop' for three specific conditions: a fire warning, an engine failure indicated by at least two parameters or a configuration warning, if for example, the flaps were at the wrong setting. As well, if the First Officer is doing the take-off, he can abort for handling difficulties or if the runway is blocked. After

rejecting a take-off, the crew would stop the jet on the runway and quickly evaluate the problem to decide if an emergency evacuation was required. Another consideration at this point is cooling the brakes. An aborted take-off near V1 at maximum weights tortures the brakes. Each brake will absorb 34 million ft lb of energy and they will require more than an hour to cool before another take-off can be attempted.

Should an engine fail on take-off, the pilots will get some help controlling the jet. Called thrust asymmetry compensation, this system assesses the thrust being produced by each engine and if it differs by 10% or more, automatically applies rudder to counter the yaw. In

keeping with Boeing's philosophy of keeping the pilot in the loop, if an engine failure occurs on the ground, the system leaves a little yaw to help the crew realise there has been a failure. In the air, the system provides all the rudder required.

As the final items of preparation, the LNAV and VNAV switches are armed. LNAV will engage at 50ft and VNAV at 400ft to guide the pilots through the flight director bars on a smooth, precise climbout.

With these preparations complete, Kevin calls for the Before Start check at 10.35Z. Referring to the electronic checklist, the flight instruments are checked set, parking brake set, fuel control switches checked CUTOFF and the proper barometric pressure set on the altimeters. The crew also select the autobrake to RTO, or rejected take-off. This arms the braking system to apply maximum brakes if the throttles are reduced to idle above 85kt on the take-off roll. As well, the spoilers will automatically deploy.

Kevin then runs through the departure briefing and highlights the actions to be taken in case of an emergency on take-off.

Captain: 'During the take-off roll advise me of any malfunctions and I will say "continue" or call "stop". Above 80 knots, I will only call stop for very serious situations. Either of us will call "stop" for any fire or any engine failure indicated by two parameters. On the call of "stop" I will close the thrust levers, disconnecting the autothrottle and verify RTO application or manually apply full braking.'

First Officer: 'At your call of stop, I will raise the reversers to the interlock, I will check the speedbrakes have deployed and if they haven't I will pull them out manually. I will then give you full reverse above 80 knots, reverse idle below 80. I will call "60 knots" as we are slowing and I'll back you up on the parking brake.'

Captain: 'Once the aircraft has been brought to a halt, I will ask you to restate the emergency and carry out any appropriate memory checklists. I will talk to the tower and the cabin as necessary and if I consider it necessary, initiate an evacuation. After V1, we'll take any problem into the air. After the gear has been selected up, restate the emergency and I will call for the appropriate checklist. Ensure that I cross-check your actions before you move any thrust lever or fuel control switch. I will engage the autopilot as soon as possible and allow the aircraft to follow the emergency turn. If we have a really significant problem, we'll return here.'

Should a problem occur on take-off, the flight will make a 15° emergency left turn to avoid a small hill southwest of the airport. Continuing with the briefing, the crew pull out the Gatwick aerodrome map books to review the SID. SIDs, or in the case of an arrival, the Standard Terminal Arrival Routeing (STAR), serve several purposes. First, by simply clearing a flight to the 'Dover Seven Victor' departure from Gatwick the controller avoids having to pass along a long-winded clearance. The crew refer to the chart to see the headings and altitude required by a SID or STAR. These published routeings also help keep departures and arrivals separated for efficient use of the airspace around a busy airport.

Today the crew can expect the Southampton Two Mike SID from Runway 26 Left. Following the SID, the flight will maintain runway heading to 8 DME from the Midhurst VOR when it will turn to 247° direct to the

Opposite above:
Graeme reviews the SID.

Opposite below:
The mode control panel on the glareshield is used to control the autopilot. For take-off, the pilots have selected the V2 speed of 155kt, a heading of 262° and an altitude of 4,000ft. The V2 speed was reduced to 153kt once load figures were received.

Right:
The door synoptic on the multi-function display shows the two front left doors and the forward and bulk cargo hatches are open.

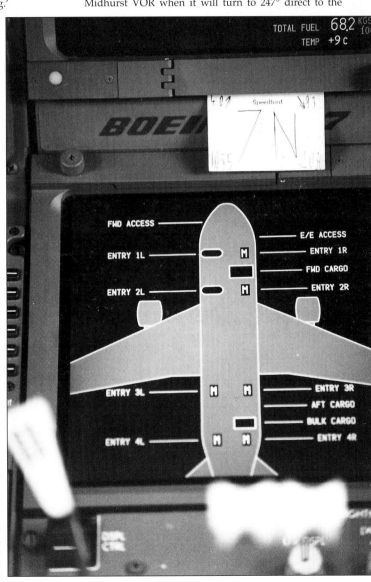

Above:
**With passengers onboard, the loading bridge
is pulled back from the aircraft.**

radio beacon. The flight will track the 261° radial from Midhurst 28nm to the VOR at Southampton. From there the crew can expect radar vectors on course. The flight must cross Midhurst at 4,000ft.

The initial heading of 262° and altitude of 4,000ft and the V2 speed of 153kt are set on the mode control panel on the glareshield. The crew check that the FMC is displaying the correct zero fuel weight of 184.8 tonnes and gross weight of 252.4 tonnes; the required take-off thrust is checked set on the EICAS; V1 and VR are confirmed correct and 'bugged' on the airspeed tape of the PFDs.

Graeme calls Gatwick delivery for their clearance to Atlanta. Though the flight number is 2227, the callsign will be 'Speedbird Seven November'. This is sometimes done to avoid any confusion with ATC if another BA flight has a similar callsign.

Gatwick Delivery: 'Speedbird Seven November for Atlanta, Southampton Two Mike departure, squawk two two two two. This frequency when you're ready for start or push.'

The 'squawk' refers to the four-digit code assigned to the flight by air traffic control. A copy of the flightplan has been filed with ATC, complete with route, requested altitudes, aircraft type and speed. ATC has assigned a code unique to this flight. This code is dialled up on the transponder on the centre console. When the plane is interrogated by radar, the transponder transmits the four-digit code as well as the aircraft's altitude. The air traffic control computer knows what code has been assigned to each IFR flight and automatically displays the jet's position, callsign, altitude and speed on the radar screen. Controllers can ask pilots to 'squawk ident'. Pushing a button on the flightdeck transponder panel causes the target to blossom briefly or flash on the radar screen, making it easier to identify.

The crew have been given the SID they expected and which they have already selected in the FMC. Although not the case today, flights departing from busy airports are sometimes given a slot time as part of their clearance which requires take-off at a certain time to facilitate traffic flows.

The door synoptic has been called up on the MFD. It shows doors 1 and 2 on the left side are open along with the forward cargo hold door as ramp crews finish loading the final pieces of cargo. The 777's two main holds, forward and aft, have a total volume of 5,056cu ft — enough to accommodate 32 LD-3 containers. A separate compartment at the rear of the aft hold has room for another 600cu ft of bulk cargo.

By now the passengers have boarded and are busily stowing carry-on bags in the spacious overhead bins and making themselves comfortable for the flight ahead with the help of the cabin staff.

With just minutes to go before departure, Kevin uses the public address to welcome everyone onboard. British Airways Flight 2227 is ready to go.

Departure

Kevin glances out his side window and watches as the loading bridge draws away from the aircraft. The ground engineer has plugged his headset into the jet's intercom system and now calls the flightdeck to inform the pilots that all doors are closed and the aircraft is ready for pushback.

Kevin asks the ground crew if it's okay to pressurise the hydraulic system. This powers the brakes for use during pushback but could also cause a gear door or flight control surface to move and Kevin wants to ensure no one is in a position where they would be hurt.

On the overhead panel, the right, left and centre hydraulic demand pumps are selected to AUTO and the centre primary pumps are switched ON. The primary pumps do most of the work and the demand pumps operate only to boost flow when there is a heavy demand on the system, such as when the landing gear is retracted.

In preparation for engine start, the fuel pumps in the right, left and centre tanks are selected ON and the beacon light switch is turned ON. Two red strobe lights on the top and bottom of the fuselage begin to flash, alerting ramp workers the jet is about to move and start engines. Kevin calls Gatwick ground control for pushback clearance.

Captain R/T: 'Ground, it's Speedbird Seven November on Gate 52 request push.'

The ground and tower controllers are located in the visual control room where they have a good view of the runway and taxiways. The ground controller organises the flow of aircraft to and from the runway. His challenge is ensuring two aircraft do not arrive nose-to-nose on a taxiway. The tower controller is responsible for the safe separation of flights in the airspace immediately around the airport and issuing clearances for take-offs and landings.

The ground controller asks the crew to stand by while he passes on instructions to three other aircraft taxiing to and from the terminal and the remote stands and then replies to Seven November's request.

Gatwick Ground: 'Seven November, inbound traffic just docking on your immediate left. After that, do a pushback to face west beyond the junction with taxiway six and you're cleared to start.'

Kevin passes on the clearance to the ground crew. Brakes are released at 10.55am — right on schedule — and a powerful tug connected to the nose gear by a towbar moves the jet away from the gate. When pushback is nearly complete, the ground crew give the okay to start engines.

The autostart feature takes all the work out of the start for the pilots. On the overhead panel, the ignition switch for the right engine is turned to START and the fuel control switch behind the throttle is moved to RUN; the

electronic engine control (EEC) looks after the rest. Compressed air from the APU is diverted from the air conditioning packs, which automatically shut off, to the starter motor in the engine which begins to spin the high pressure shaft, known as N2.

At 22% N2, there is sufficient air in the combustion section for a start. The fuel valves open automatically, fuel begins flowing and one of two ignition systems on the engine begins firing to supply the spark to start combustion. On the EICAS display, the EGT is seen to rise rapidly and a deep rumble is heard as the massive GE90-85B engine fires up. Exiting the engine, the hot exhaust gases spin a series of turbine blades connected to the low pressure shaft, referred to as N1, that drives the front fan blades. These large blades begin to turn, drawing in more air to sustain combustion. Within 2min, engine combustion is self-sufficient and the igniters stop firing. The engine settles into idle at 22% N1, a fuel flow of 900kg/hr and showing an EGT of 513° Celsius. The left engine is started in similar fashion.

The only action required of the crew during the start is to confirm a rise in oil pressure on the secondary engine indications which are shown on the lower display during start. The electronic engine control automatically corrects for a number of problems that can occur, like a hot start when the exhaust gas temperatures rise above limits. If the first start attempt fails, the EEC will automatically motor the engine briefly to clear it of excess fuel, then try another start using the other set of igniters. Should that attempt fail, it will try once more using both ignition systems. In flight, continuous

Below:
The upper EICAS display before engine start. The top dials show the N1 speed for each engine and EGT is shown below. The 96.6 displayed above each N1 gauge is the selected take-off thrust. The total fuel load is displayed in the bottom right corner. The tall stack of warning and alert messages will disappear once the engines are running.

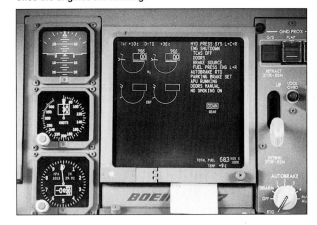

Above:
With pushback nearly complete, the pilots await the okay from the ground crew to start engines.

check for any outstanding EICAS messages. These messages can be cleared from the screen if the situation does not require immediate action. Pressing the recall button on the glareshield will display those outstanding EICAS messages and warnings that still require action.

Captain R/T: 'Ground, it's Speedbird Seven November ready for taxi.'

Gatwick Ground: 'Seven November roger, follow the 747 onto taxiway six, QNH is one zero two one.'

As noted from the ATIS, the active runway is 26 Left. Runways are numbered according to their magnetic bearing rounded off to the nearest 10°. The actual heading of this runway is 262°. The opposite end is marked for the reciprocal heading, in this case Runway 08 Right. Parallel runways are marked 'L' or 'R' for left

ignition is manually selected during conditions that can cause engine flame-out, such as heavy rain, icing conditions and severe turbulence. As well, continuous ignition automatically activates when engine anti-ice is on or the flaps are deployed.

When the pushback is complete, the ground team calls for the parking brake to be set. Kevin pushes on the toe pedals and pulls up on the parking brake handle on the centre console. He confirms on the intercom that brakes are set but the ground crew can check for themselves thanks to a new feature on the 777. Lights on the nose gear show when brakes are applied and the parking brake set.

Captain intercom: 'Thank you ground, that's two good starts. Confirm all the ground equipment away and pins removed please.'

This latter comment refers to the steering lockout pin which is inserted in the nose gear prior to pushback so it can swing freely without damaging the steering mechanism. From the right window, the crew watch the ramp crew and tug move clear of the aircraft.

The crew run through the After Start checklist: the APU is turned OFF, engine anti-ice selectors are confirmed set to AUTO.

The anti-ice protection would be turned on if the temperature was below 10° Celsius and there was precipitation falling, a wet runway or fog. The crew also

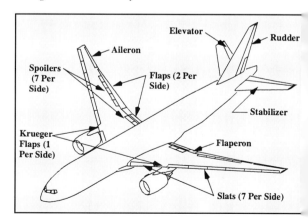

or right. Despite their size, commercial jets still make take-offs and landings into the wind. A headwind on take-off reduces the distance required to get airborne while a 10kt tailwind on landing can add 1,000ft to the rollout of a Boeing 777.

Before the jet moves, each pilot looks out of his side window and confirms there are no obstacles. Taxying an aircraft this size requires a careful touch. The crew cannot see the wingtips and being perched high above the tarmac, there is a large area where personnel and equipment are hidden from view.

Kevin releases the brakes and lets the aircraft move forward on idle thrust alone. The huge fan on the GE90 provides ample idle thrust, making the aircraft eager to taxi. Even at high weights, it will begin rolling without applying power. In fact, during tests a 777 with GE engines got up to 38kt on just idle thrust. For that reason, flight crews have to use caution. Even at low power, the exhaust blast from the large, high bypass engines is strong enough to damage ground equipment and injure staff. No more than 30% N1 is recommended for taxying.

Kevin steers the jet left onto taxiway six and follows a British Airways 747-400 to Runway 26 Left. Each pilot has the Gatwick aerodrome chart clipped just below the side windows for easy reference. Gatwick has a simple layout but some airports are a virtual maze of taxiways, making ground operations a challenge, especially in low visibility.

The 777 is supported by two huge main gear bogies — each with three axles and six wheels rather than the conventional four-wheel units — and a two-wheel nose gear. The rationale behind the extra wheels was to provide better weight distribution on runways and taxiways and avoid the need for an extra two-wheel unit under the fuselage.

The jet is steered using one of the tillers on both sides of the cockpit which move the nosewheel 70° in either direction. In tighter turns, the aft axles on the main gear turn up to 8° in either direction to reduce the turning radius and tyre scrubbing. It is activated automatically whenever the nosewheel turns more than 13°. To make a 180° turn, the jet requires pavement at least 160ft wide. The main gear is 92ft behind the flightdeck and the pilots have to deliberately overshoot turns to keep the wheels out of the grass. The longer 777-300 is equipped with cameras to show the position of the main wheels and nose gear on flightdeck displays.

Moving along taxiway six, 'India Juliet' passes the west park, a collection of remote stands. On the left side, aircraft are parked at the gates of the South Terminal.

Opposite below:
The flight controls. *British Airways*

Above:
Flap 15 is selected for take-off. Both the outboard aileron and the flaperon on each wing droop down to improve lift during take-off.

Gatwick Ground: 'Speedbird Seven November, give way to the ATR (turboprop) to pass between you and the 747 and then continue into Alpha three.'

Kevin calls for Flap 15 to initiate the Before Take-Off check. Graeme moves the flap lever back and watches as the EICAS display shows the flaps moving the desired setting. The 777 has a single-slotted outboard flap and a double-slotted inboard flap on each wing. Located between the inboard and outboard flaps is a flaperon which works as both an aileron and flap. The flaperons

BEFORE START

INT/EXT SECURITY CHECK . . . . COMPLETE

OXYGEN. . . . . CHECKED

PASSENGER SIGNS . . . . .SET

FLIGHT INSTRUMENTS .SET

QNH . . . . .SET

AUTOBRAKE . . . . RTO

PARKING BRAKE . . . . .SET

FUEL CONTROL SWITCHES . . . . .CUTOFF

BRIEFING: MEL/STATUS. AIS, rwy state, sig weather. Emergencies, performance restrictions, terrain clearance, return alternate. SID, radio aids, transition altitude, AFDS (LNAV, VNAV, hdg, alt).

FMC. . . . . .SET

T/O THRUST. . . . . .SET

REF SPEEDS . . . . .SET

LNAV/VNAV . . . . .SET

CLEARED FOR START

HYDRAULIC PANEL . . . . .SET

FUEL PANEL . . . . .SET

BEACON. . . . . ON

DOORS (prior to push back) . . . . .CLOSED

RECALL . . . . CHECKED

AFTER START

APU SELECTOR . . . . .AS REQUIRED

ENGINE ANTI-ICE . . . . .AS REQUIRED

RECALL . . . . CHECKED

GROUND ENGINEERS CLEARANCE. . . . . . RECEIVED

BEFORE TAKEOFF

VITAL DATA . . . . .SET

FLAPS. . . . . .___

FLIGHT CONTROLS . . . . CHECKED

TRIMS. . . . . .SET

TRANSPONDER. . . . . .SET

CABIN CREW REPORT. . . . . RECEIVED

...Entering Runway...

EXTERIOR LIGHTS . . . . .AS REQUIRED

CABIN CREW SIGNAL . . . . GIVEN

AFTER TAKEOFF

LANDING GEAR. . . . . .UP

FLAPS. . . . . .UP

ENGINE ANTI-ICE . . . . AUTO

...Transition Altitude...

ALTIMETERS . . . . .SET

DESCENT BRIEFING

Safety altitudes - Transition level - AIS - U/S items. Recall, Notes - Sig weather - STAR - Approach - Minima - Radio aids. R/W state - Reverse - Brakes - Airfield - Go-around - Diversion.

DESCENT/APPROACH

RECALL AND NOTES . . . . CHECKED

BRIEFING. . . . . CONFIRMED

MINIMA . . . . .SET

AUTOBRAKE . . . . .SET

VREF. . . . . .SET

...Transition Level...

ALTIMETERS . . . . .SET

LANDING

SPEEDBRAKE. . . . . ARMED

LANDING GEAR . . . . DOWN

FLAPS . . . . .___

CABIN CREW REPORT. . . . . .RECEIVED

AFTER LANDING

STROBES. . . . . OFF

SPEEDBRAKE. . . . . DOWN

FLAPS . . . . .UP

WEATHER RADAR . . . . OFF

TRANSPONDER .TCAS OFF

APU ELECTRICS . . . . AVAILABLE

...Approaching Stand...

DOORS. . . . . MANUAL

SHUTDOWN

HYDRAULIC PANEL . . . . .SET

FUEL PUMP SWITCHES . . . .,. . . . . OFF

PARKING BRAKE . . . . .SET

FUEL CONTROL SWITCHES . . . . .CUTOFF

SECURE

ADIRU SWITCH . . . . OFF

BATTERY SWITCH. . . . . OFF

EMERGENCY LIGHTS SWITCH . . . . OFF

PACK SWITCHES . . . . OFF

BRITISH AIRWAYS

B777

6 OCTOBER 1997

NC-01

ATP 3123/NC

move down and aft as flaps are extended to increase lift while continuing to work as ailerons to provide roll control.

The outboard ailerons assist with low-speed handling and are locked out at about 270kt. They also droop with the selection of Flaps 5, 15 and 20 to improve take-off performance. They return to a neutral setting when landing flap settings are selected. Seven spoiler panels on each wing can operate independently to assist roll control or together as speedbrakes. At higher speeds, ailerons and two spoilers are locked out and roll control is provided by the flaperons and remaining spoilers.

Continuing with the checklist, the First Officer moves the control column left and right and front and back to confirm full travel of the controls and their return to neutral. The rudder is also displaced left and right by the Captain. Aileron and rudder trims are confirmed set at zero and stabiliser trim checked set at 4.5 units.

Cabin Service Director Mark Howden enters the flightdeck and advises the cabin is ready for departure. The lead-up to departure has been a busy time for the 13 cabin crew. Prior to the passengers boarding, they performed a security check of the cabin and confirmed all safety equipment was in place. They then prepared the cabin for the passengers and stowed the food and beverage carts brought on board by catering staff. As the aircraft moves out to the runway, a video highlighting the safety features of the aircraft is played on monitors throughout the cabin. The cabin doors have been set to automatic. Should an evacuation be required now, emergency chutes would automatically deploy when the doors were opened, allowing passengers and crew to slide to safety. Certification tests required Boeing to demonstrate the 777 could be safely evacuated in 90sec or less using only four of the plane's eight doors, with the cabin lights extinguished and suitcases strewn in the aisles to simulate a real emergency.

A chime sounds on the flightdeck, alerting the crew to the arrival of the final load figures via the datalink. The take-off weight is now 251,300kg, just slightly less than the original figure, and there are 152 passengers onboard, 12 fewer than expected. The new numbers are within the margins of the original figures and do not change the take-off performance data already done by the crew.

Entering a holding bay adjacent to the runway, Kevin stops the jet using the toe pedals to apply carbon brakes on the main gear. At low speeds, braking is alternated

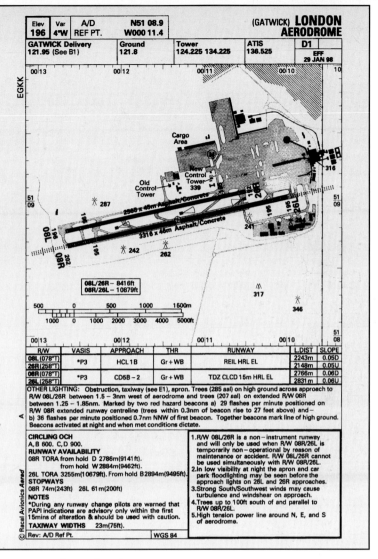

Opposite:
The Boeing 777 checklists. *British Airways*

Above:
The Gatwick aerodrome chart. *Racal Avionics*

between four of the six brakes on each truck to reduce brake wear.

The crew check in on the tower frequency of 124.22 MHz. The controller asks them to taxi past the 747-400 they had followed from the terminal. They are now number two in line behind another British Airways 747-400 that has just been cleared for take-off.

Gatwick Tower: 'Speedbird Seven November, after the departing 747, position two six left.'

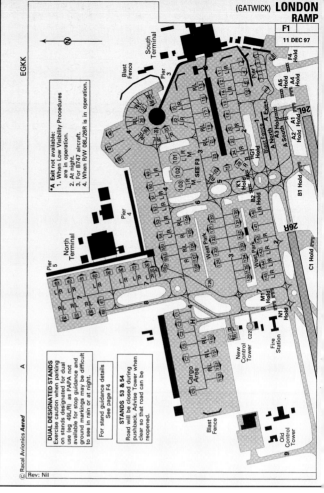

Graeme reaches to the overhead panel and turns on the strobe and landing lights and sounds a chime in the cabin to alert the crew that the take-off roll is about to commence. The pilots ensure no aircraft is on late finals and double-check the TCAS returns on the ND for any landing traffic, a good tool when low cloud prevents a visual check. Kevin taxies the Boeing 777 out of the holding bay and onto the runway, turning the jet to the right to line up with the centreline. Looking down the 10,879ft runway, the crew watch as the Boeing 747-400 rotates and takes to the air bound for Miami.

Gatwick Tower: 'Speedbird Seven November, surface wind is two two zero degrees at eight knots, you're cleared take-off two six.'

At 11.06Z, British Airways Flight 2227 is on its way. Kevin releases the brakes and advances the throttles to 55% N1. He lets the engines stabilise momentarily — Graeme says 'Engines stable' — before pushing the take-off/go-around buttons (TO/GA) buttons on the front of the throttles. This causes the autothrottle to advance the thrust levers to the target power setting of 96.6% N1.

The whine of the engines becomes a roar. When take-off thrust is achieved, Graeme calls 'power set'. The acceleration presses the crew and passengers firmly in their seats. Kevin's left hand is on the control column

Above left:
A British Airways 747-400 begins its take-off roll and Speedbird Seven November is cleared into position on the runway.

Above:
The diagram showing the layout of Gatwick's runways and taxiways is kept close at hand during the taxi. The flight has been cleared from Gate 52 along taxiway six to Runway 26 Left. *Racal Avionics*

Left:
Cleared for take-off. Kevin advances the throttles and Graeme confirms power is set. The big jet accelerates down the runway.

and he keeps the jet on the centreline using the rudder pedals, which are connected to the nosewheel. The rudder becomes effective between 40 and 60kt. His right hand is on the throttles, ready to cut the power should the take-off have to be aborted.

During the roll, Graeme is watching the engine readouts and cross-checking the airspeed indications. He calls '80 knots'. Now they will stop for only a serious emergency that would threaten the jet's ability to fly.

At 148kt, an automated voice calls 'Vee one'. Graeme calls 'rotate' and Kevin pulls smoothly back on the control column. The ideal rotation rate is 2.5° per second. Rotating too slowly eats up runway and a rapid rotation could cause the aft fuselage to strike the runway. Even during a normal take-off, the fuselage clears the pavement by as little as 3ft.

The jet is airborne in about 5,600ft. After lift-off, Kevin follows the flight director bars on the PFD to an initial pitch attitude of 15°, climbing at V2 + 15kt. This is the optimum climb speed with take-off flaps and gives the maximum altitude gain in the shortest distance.

Passing 100ft above ground, Graeme calls 'positive rate,' confirming that the jet is safely established in the climb. Kevin responds 'gear up' and the First Officer reaches forward and moves the gear lever up. Brakes automatically apply to stop wheel spin, gear doors open and the main and nose wheels are retracted into the fuselage. With the aircraft cleaned up, the noise level on the flightdeck drops considerably.

The magenta flight director bars are guiding Kevin along the flight profile required by the SID and at 1,000ft the horizontal bar moves down to command a lower pitch attitude, allowing the aircraft to accelerate for flap retraction. The power automatically retards to climb power, about 89% N1.

The FMC has automatically calculated the flap retraction speeds which are displayed on the airspeed tape. The speed is increasing now and through 1,800ft the flaps are raised in quick succession. Kevin calls first for Flap 5, then Flap 1. At this setting, the trailing edge flaps retract completely leaving only the leading edge slats extended. As the aircraft passes 200kt, flaps up is selected to retract the slats.

Gatwick Tower: 'Speedbird Seven November, contact London Control one three four decimal one two, good day.'

Graeme tunes the new frequency and checks in with the radar controller working the southwest terminal sector whose job it is to guide the flight through the arrivals. The typical solution is to restrict the climbs of outbound aircraft until they are clear of the inbound jets. During busy times, this position is split into two, one controller for Gatwick arrivals and one for departures.

First Officer R/T: 'London good morning it's Speedbird Seven November passing two thousand three hundred on Southampton Two Mike.'

London Control: 'Speedbird Seven November, there's no speed restriction, you're cleared to flight level one hundred.'

The new altitude of 10,000 is dialled into the mode control panel and Kevin presses the autopilot button, engaging all three autopilot channels. The FMC commands a climb speed below 10,000ft of 250kt or flaps-up manoeuvring speed (Vref + 80kt), whichever is greater, to comply with ATC restrictions. But with no

Top:
Airborne! At Kevin's call, Graeme selects gear up and the wheels retract into the fuselage. Next stop is Atlanta.

Above:
The ND shows the flight over the Southampton VOR. The track line ahead is intersected by a green arc showing where the flight will reach the altitude selected on the mode control panel. Further along the track just before the waypoint SWANY is the symbol T/C, or top of climb. This marks where the jet will level at its cruising altitude if permitted to climb unrestricted by ATC. The TCAS function is showing the 747 that departed just ahead of the Atlanta flight.

restriction, the aircraft can accelerate to its most efficient climb speed of 320kt, just 10kt short of the maximum indicated airspeed. The jet is climbing at 2,300ft per minute.

The flight has been in broken cloud since 2,000ft. But passing 5,700ft, it bursts into blue sky and the cloud layer drops away, prompting Graeme to remark: 'Best part of the day.' That's the one good thing about being an airline pilot, regardless of the weather on the ground, they're usually guaranteed some blue sky in their working day.

London Control: 'Speedbird Seven November fly heading of two seven zero degrees.'

For some reason, most likely because of traffic ahead, the controller is vectoring the flight off the SID. Kevin cancels LNAV and dials in 270 on the heading window of the mode control panel and selects HDG, or heading mode. The autopilot turns the jet on to the new course.

There are four air traffic control centres in the United Kingdom: Manchester Area Control Centre, London Air Traffic Control Centre, the Scottish Air Traffic Control Centre and the Oceanic Area Control Centre, these last two both located at Prestwick, Scotland.

The crew are now under the control of the London ATCC, the largest of the control centres, which is located at West Drayton just north of Heathrow. In 1997, London handled a record 1,577,906 flights, a 6% increase over 1996. During the winter, daily totals average about 4,000 flights. That grows to just under 5,000 flights a day during the busy summer season. The centre is divided into two components. London Terminal control is responsible for flights in the southeast of England up to 17,000ft. Area control has jurisdiction over a much larger parcel of airspace that stretches from Holland to Ireland and from France to the Scottish border. In the southern section of this airspace, area controllers handle traffic above 17,000ft while in the north, beyond the boundaries of London Terminal, their jurisdiction drops to about 5,000ft and above.

About 600 controllers work out of the centre and at any one time about 60 controllers are working area control and another 40 are staffing the terminal positions.

Within several years, the facility at West Drayton will be replaced by a new en route air traffic control centre at Swanwick, near Fareham, Hampshire. When it goes into service, ATC staff say Swanwick will be the largest and most technologically advanced control centre in the world. Its operations room will cover an area of 2,000sq m and will be designed to handle up to 45 sectors of airspace. It is expected the improved technology and airspace realignment will result in a 40% increase in en route capacity. However, problems with the complex software has delayed the start of operations at the centre and the expected launch date has been pushed back to the winter of 1999-2000. First to move will be the area controllers, followed three to four years after that by the terminal staff.

Above:
Air traffic control has lifted a speed restriction, allowing the jet to climb at an efficient 320kt, giving a climb rate of 2,300fpm.
John M. Dibbs

Below:
Graeme has plotted the jet's route on a flight progress chart and he shows it to the Captain for review.

The controller turns the flight left to 260° and clears them to 15,000ft. Through 10,000ft, the landing lights are turned off and Kevin calls 'altimeter check'. Graeme responds 'flight level one hundred, climbing flight level one five zero, standard set'.

The crew have selected the standard barometric pressure setting on the altimeters. Once the flight is 'clean' — clear of the arrivals — it is handed off to the en route controller. This transition facilitates a continuous climb. The aim is to prevent the wasteful move of having to level off during the climb to altitude. The flight is handed off to London Control on 135.05MHz.

First Officer R/T: 'London, Speedbird Seven November with you passing flight level one one five for flight level one five zero.'

The controller responds with a request to turn left to 245° and after a few minutes calls back with clearance to 25,000ft. The crew are with this controller for only a short time before they are transferred to the controller working the Berry Head sector, named after a point of land near Torbay.

London Control: 'Speedbird Seven November, turn right heading two six zero degrees and report your new heading to London on one two six decimal zero seven, bye, bye.'

The next controller clears the flight to FL280. Fifteen minutes after take-off, the jet passes FL230, climbing at 1,150 fpm. The wind arrow on the ND shows the wind blowing from 204° at 29kt, giving a groundspeed of 483kt.

At this point, it is necessary to call Shanwick for confirmation of their oceanic clearance. Shanwick is the ATC agency that oversees oceanic airspace from the 45th parallel north to the 60th parallel and out to 30° West, about half-way across the Atlantic. Kevin keeps an ear on ATC while Graeme tunes the frequency for Shanwick. In his radio call, Graeme provides the co-ordinates of the flight's entry into oceanic airspace, their ETA to that waypoint and their desired flight level and cruising speed for the crossing.

First Officer R/T: 'Shanwick, it's Speedbird Seven November, good

morning, requesting oceanic clearance, oceanic entry point is five five north, one zero west at one two one three, flight level three seven zero, Mach decimal eight four.'

Shanwick Clearance: 'Roger Speedbird Seven November, stand by.'

The frequency is busy as other transatlantic flights check in for their clearances. The westbound rush is under way and controllers are jockeying dozens of flights headed to coastal waypoints that serve as entry points to the Oceanic Control Area.

Controllers are organising the aircraft on to their assigned tracks and establishing the separations that will keep the jets safely apart on their ocean crossing. Aircraft at the same altitude on the same track are spaced 10min apart. The spacing can be reduced to 5min if the first aircraft arriving at an oceanic entry point is flying at least Mach 0.06 faster than the one behind it. Proper separation is based on accurate ETAs; flight crews must advise ATC if their ETA to a waypoint changes by 3min or more.

The crew listen in as the 747-400 flight that departed ahead of them from Gatwick receives its clearance. Then Shanwick is calling the Atlanta flight.

Shanwick Clearance: 'Shanwick clears Speedbird Seven November to Atlanta via Track Foxtrot from five five north, one zero west, maintain flight level three seven zero, Mach decimal eight four.'

Graeme repeats the clearance and at the end of the transmission, rhymes off that day's track identifier number. This tells ATC that the pilots have a copy of the day's tracks and spares them a long-winded readback of each waypoint on their designated path across the ocean.

Shanwick Clearance: 'Roger Speedbird Seven November, continue now on domestic frequency, good day.'

Right:
Half an hour after take-off, the flight has just a few hundred feet left to climb to reach its initial cruising altitude of FL350.

The flight has been cleared as filed and since the routeing is already in the FMC, the crew is spared making any changes. A change in tracks can make for a busy time punching the new waypoints into the FMC.

While Graeme was getting the oceanic clearance, ATC cleared the flight to FL290 and direct to EXMOR, a waypoint on the south side of the Bristol Channel. Using the CDU, Kevin selects this as the active waypoint in the FMC. The aircraft turns to a heading of 311° for EXMOR where it will pick up airway UR14. The crew had been handling the many course changes through HDG mode. Kevin activates LNAV and the autopilot now flies the route programmed in the FMC with no further intervention by the pilots.

At 11.28Z, the flight levels at FL290 and Graeme checks in with a new controller on 133.6.

First Officer R/T: 'Speedbird Seven November good morning, level two niner zero.'

London Control: 'Speedbird Seven November roger, what is your requested level?'

First Officer R/T: 'Level three five zero, Speedbird Seven November.'

London Control: 'Speedbird Seven November climb flight level three five zero.'

The new altitude is reached at 11.38Z. The climb, with some stops along the way, has taken 31min, consumed 6.3 tonnes of fuel and covered 184nm. The jet settles into cruise at Mach 0.838. The indicated airspeed is 286kt and the true airspeed, corrected for air density and temperature, is 476kt. A wind blowing from 227° at 50kt gives a groundspeed of 493kt.

It has been a busy half hour for the pilots but now, with the aircraft at altitude and oceanic clearance in hand, they can relax somewhat for the long flight ahead. Atlanta is 3,671nm away.

Above
The ECON CRZ page of the FMC suggests the best altitudes to fly at. At this point, the maximum altitude they can reach at the jet's current weight is 38,000ft. The optimum altitude based on weight is 35,000ft which also happens to be the recommended altitude for the winds aloft. Also on this page, the FMC is predicting the flight will arrive at 20.01Z with 9.8 tonnes of fuel onboard.

Below:
The crew settle in for the flight ahead.

En Route

'Here, all around me, is the Atlantic — its expanse, its depth, its power, its wild and open water. Is there something unique about this ocean that gives it character above all other seas, or is it my imagination?'
Charles Lindbergh, in his book *Spirit of St Louis*

The airway UR14 doglegs to the northwest at the Strumble VOR and British Airways Flight 2227 turns to stay on it, taking up a new course of 334° to Dublin.

At 11.41Z, control of the jet is transferred to Shannon Control on 132.15MHz. Checking in, Graeme receives clearance to fly direct to 5510N for the start of the ocean crossing. The new routeing shaves miles and minutes off the original route.

With the departure behind them, the workload has eased considerably. Though ocean crossings are usually quiet, there is still work to be done. The main chore is monitoring the jet's progress and ensuring times and fuel burns on each leg are in line with the expectations set out in the flightplan. The pilots work out a schedule that will give each of them a 2hr break and at 11.55Z, Rehman slips back to a seat in business class for his rest period.

Crossing Ireland, which is masked by a carpet of cloud, the flight is cleared to FL370, the altitude it will maintain until the far side of the ocean. Mark Howden, the Cabin Service Director, visits the flightdeck to advise Kevin he has a few moments to speak to the passengers before the movies start.

Captain PA: 'Good morning, it's the Captain, Kevin Mottram. Just before the in-flight entertainment gets underway, I'd like to give you some information about the route. Currently at our cruising altitude of thirty seven thousand feet just coming up over the northwest coast of Ireland. Our routeing today will take us quite far north and eventually we will pass just south of Greenland and then make our landfall on the Canadian coast near Goose Bay. Our route takes us down following the St Lawrence Seaway, crossing into the United States, passing to the west of Boston, New York

Above right:
The main chore now is keeping vigil over the jet's progress across the ocean and its fuel consumption.

Right:
With the workload of pre-flight and departure behind them, the pilots work out a rest schedule for the trip.

```
/AMET BIKF
SA 061130   23025KT 9999 VCSH SCT013CB BKN040
02/M05 Q0974
            20290063 -

FC 061100   061221 24018G30KT 9999 FEW012CB
SCT040 TEMPO 1221
            1500 SHSN BKN004 BECMG 1821
20012KT -
```

Left:
Graeme uses ACARS to get updated weather conditions for en route airports. The report from BIKF — Keflavik, Iceland — shows okay weather but strong winds.

Above:
Boeing says the 777 wing is the most aerodynamically efficient wing ever developed for subsonic commercial aviation. A refinement of the design introduced on the 757 and 767, it features a long span with increased thickness and achieves higher cruise speeds.
John M. Dibbs

Right:
The engines draw fuel from the centre tank until it runs low about an hour into the flight. Graeme switches off the fuel pumps for that tank and the engines begin using fuel from the two main tanks.

and down to Atlanta where our computers are predicting we will land twenty five minutes ahead of schedule. Weather in Atlanta is forecast to be fine. I hope you enjoy your flight with us and I'll talk to you later. Thank you.'

Control of the flight is handed off to Scottish Control on 125.675MHz.

The FMC provides all of the required cruise information and ETAs to the various waypoints are easily read off the progress page. Although still early in the flight, the FMC is predicting 9.8 tonnes of fuel remaining upon landing, a healthy margin over the 7.5 tonnes of diversion and reserve fuel required. The FMC is also predicting an arrival time of 20.01Z, a half-hour ahead of schedule.

Should an engine fail now, the crew would select the ENG OUT prompt on the aircraft cruise page of the FMC. This would call up the engine-out driftdown altitude, in this case 20,500ft. This is the highest altitude the aircraft could maintain on one engine at the current weight. It would be set in the altitude window of the mode control panel and the crew would execute the descent in the FMC. The remaining engine would increase power to maximum continuous thrust and the autopilot would start a gradual descent to the selected altitude and slow to the long-range, engine-out cruise speed, which would be Mach 0.5 or about 279kt indicated airspeed at this altitude. The FMC also informs the crew there is insufficient fuel to reach Atlanta cruising on a single engine. Not that the crew would complete the trip on one engine but it does show the variety of information they have at their fingertips.

Just before the plane leaves VHF range, Graeme checks the navigation accuracy. On the ND, he calls up the individual positions generated by radio aids, the FMC and the GPS systems and ensures all are within tolerance. He also uses the datalink to get the latest weather reports for the diversionary airfields to ensure conditions remain good enough for a diversion and landing. During the crossing, weather information is broadcast on high frequency radio from New York, Gander and Shannon for a variety of airfields. While the crew of any flight likes to have the most up-to-date weather information, it is especially vital for an ETOPS flight. If they suffer an engine failure, they do not have the luxury of continuing a flight to the destination — they are required to land at the nearest diversionary airfield.

Today's destination of Atlanta does not often get hit by snow storms but crews are especially vigilant when flying to cities along the eastern seaboard like New York or Boston during the winter. Severe frontal weather can bring all the airports to a standstill, causing significant disruptions as aircraft seek out diversion airports with better weather. The weather systems do not have to be widespread to snarl traffic. A storm hitting the New York area alone would be enough to slow hundreds of flights in and out of Newark, LaGuardia and Kennedy airports. British Airways does not permit landings on runways with deep standing water, deep snow or deep slush unless diversion is impractical. When bad weather is forecast, the general rule is to have a well-thought-out diversion plan and plenty of reserve fuel.

At 12.01Z, the crew note the message 'FUEL LOW CENTRE' on the EICAS display. Just 0.7 tonnes of fuel remain in the centre tank, down from 10.4 tonnes at the start of flight. Fuel in the centre tank is used first because the two pumps in this tank have a higher output pressure than the pumps in the two main tanks. When the centre tank is down to 0.5 tonnes of fuel, Graeme turns off its fuel pumps. The engines now draw from the main tanks, fed by two boost pumps in each tank. Apart from monitoring fuel levels for the rest of the trip, this is the only action required of the crew to manage the fuel system. The remaining fuel in the centre tank is automatically transferred to the main tanks by a scavenge pump.

Ten minutes later, the flight passes 5510N and enters oceanic airspace. With the push of a button, the crew switch the heading reference to the true north pole from magnetic north pole, which is actually several hundred miles away from the true north pole. The difference between the two is called variation and this has to be factored in when using magnetic headings for navigation. However, at these latitudes the magnetic variation is large and changes rapidly over short distances so true heading is used instead.

The crew is now talking via high frequency radio to Shanwick Radio, the agency responsible for air traffic control over the eastern half of the ocean. The people talking to the flights are not controllers but rather radio operators located near Shannon, Ireland. The operators relay the information to oceanic controllers at the control centre at Prestwick, Scotland. The involvement of the two agencies explains the 'Shanwick' callsign.

It is almost an anachronism to find HF radios still being used on an aircraft as sophisticated as the 777. Yet VHF radios are restricted by line of sight and are only good until about 200 miles offshore when reception drops off. That is when the high frequency radios, for all their hiss and crackle, prove their mettle by providing communications over hundreds and thousands of miles.

HF radios will continue in use for some years yet until satcom systems become commonplace.

Graeme calls Shanwick radio to request a SELCAL check, short for selective calling system, and provides the radio operator with the aircraft's unique code, GK-FR. The SELCAL system enables ATC to ring individual aircraft and saves the flight crew from having to keep a listening watch. A two-tone chime sounds on the flightdeck signalling a successful test and the pilots hang up their headsets knowing ATC can reach them if necessary.

The emergency frequency of 121.5MHz is tuned on the right VHF radio and 131.8 on the left. This is a chit-chat frequency which pilots flying the ocean use to exchange reports of turbulence and weather information.

The ND shows that 5720N, the next waypoint, is 356nm away and will be reached at 12.59Z. The engines are turning at 92% N1 and are consuming 3.9 tonnes of fuel an hour each. The wind is blowing from 238° at 65kt, giving the jet a groundspeed of 450kt. Autothrottle response is reduced during cruise to minimise throttle activity and, as a result, it will permit significant speed changes even up to Mach 0.87 — the maximum allowable — before commanding a power change. Boeing 777 pilots must take care to avoid overspeeds when experiencing airspeed fluctuations due to turbulence, even if it means slowing slightly to Mach 0.82.

A glance out the flightdeck windows reveals nothing but empty blue sky. In fact, this is busy airspace: in 1997, controllers in Gander handled some 270,000 oceanic flights, up by about 7% over the previous year. The Scottish Oceanic Area Control Centre predicts its operations to grow to 365,000 flights a year by 2009.

The oceanic airspace is congested primarily for two reasons: transatlantic flights are concentrated within a short time period and they prefer to fly in a narrow band of altitudes where fuel economy is best.

This congestion has prompted a new procedure, known as reduced vertical separation minima (RVSM), that enables flights to fly more efficient routes and provides greater capacity to meet future demand over the North Atlantic. The vertical separation between aircraft above FL290 is normally 2,000ft but RVSM doubles the number of flight levels available by reducing separation to 1,000ft on the oceanic tracks. Safety standards are maintained by improvements in the accuracy of altimeters and the procedure is open only to those aircraft equipped with altimetry systems that meet certain performance specifications.

The first westbound aircraft to use the new procedure was a United Airlines Boeing 777 en route from Paris to Washington.

The programme was initially introduced between 33,000 and 37,000ft with aircraft spaced at FL340, 350, 360 and 370. It was expanded in the autumn of 1998 to include the airspace between FL320 and FL380.

Oceanic controllers describe the programme as a 'win-win'. For pilots, the procedure means a better chance of getting their first choice of altitude, speed and track for the Atlantic crossing. With the growing amount of traffic, it was not always possible for flights to operate at their optimum altitudes which results in higher fuel burn. It is estimated the procedure will save airlines £20 million a year by 2015. With the extra flight levels,

The view from the Captain's seat level at 37,000ft over the Atlantic Ocean — blue sky and smooth air.

controllers are able to handle the traffic with one or two fewer oceanic tracks, freeing airspace for random routeings. These are used by jets flying to destinations that make it inefficient to fly on the ocean tracks. The North Atlantic was chosen by the International Civil Aviation Organisation as the proving ground for RVSM because it would bring immediate benefits to this congested airspace but use of this procedure is expected to spread to other parts of the world.

The reduced separation makes for some rather dramatic encounters and while safe, the sight of a Boeing 747 flying 1,000ft overhead is eye-catching. The crew of BA 2227 listen in on one radio exchange as the pilot of a United Airlines flight alerts the crew of another flight they are about to pass below. 'Is my gear up?' quips the pilot of the jet being overtaken. 'No, but your plane's belly is really dirty,' the United pilot jokingly responds.

Back on the flightdeck, Kevin is conversing with airline staff in London on the topic of 777 performance figures. As technical manager for the 777 fleet, Kevin has many responsibilities and these continue to keep him busy, even far from the office, high above the Atlantic. Because the 777 is new to Gatwick, operations staff are just finalising performance numbers for the airport. Thanks to the jet's satcom system, Kevin is able to give his input on the issue. The system works much like a telephone and has 100 numbers stored in its memory, allowing the crew to call various departments in British Airways such as the medical director, operations and maintenance for assistance in solving in-flight problems. It is an invaluable tool, especially when out of VHF range. The satcom system has five voice channels and one for the datalink. Passengers can make long-distance calls on the system as well, but at a price.

Satellite communications and satellite navigation, 84,700lb jet engines — this flight is a world away from the Vickers Vanguard in which Kevin started his flying career in 1971 with British European Airways, a predecessor of British Airways. Those early days were spent flying not passengers but cargo on one of the many four-engined turboprop Vanguards the airline had converted to freighters.

In the years since, he has enjoyed a colourful career with the airline. From the Vanguard he moved to British Airtours to fly the Boeing 707 on charter flights to the Mediterranean, Los Angeles and Australia. He then flew the BAC 1-11 for four years on short-haul routes out of Heathrow. He also flew the jet with British Airways on domestic German flights out of Berlin to Hanover, Cologne and Stuttgart, all flown below 10,000ft because of the airspace restrictions in place at the time in East Germany.

He transferred to the Lockheed L-1011 where he became a captain and was appointed Flight Manager, Technical, of the TriStar fleet in 1989. It was in that position that he had the privilege of flying some of Britain's top names to destinations around the world. He flew the former Prime Minister John Major to Hong Kong, HM Queen Elizabeth II to New Zealand and TRH The Prince and Princess of Wales to South America. For those flights, the aircraft was taken out of service two weeks beforehand to have the royal kit installed. The business class was moved to tourist class to accommodate the entourage that travels with the royals. The first class area was reconfigured as a royal suite complete with a sitting area and two bedrooms.

Kevin was appointed to the Boeing 777 programme in 1991 — shortly after the project was launched — and transferred to the 747-400 to become familiar with the Boeing flightdeck layout and design philosophy.

As one of the top managers on the aircraft, there is no shortage of paperwork and administrative duties to keep him busy at the Compass Centre, the airline's operations hub at Heathrow. Still, he flies as often as his office schedule allows, to keep his finger on the fun and challenges of day-to-day line flying. (In fact, two months after this flight, Kevin returned to the line full-time.)

Graeme joined the airline 10 years earlier after flying helicopters with the Royal Australian Navy. During this time with the navy he logged 1,845 deck landings, including almost 500 at night, on everything from aircraft carriers to frigates, and was promoted to Lieutenant Commander. Since joining the airline, he has flown the 737-200 and -400, the 757, 767 and now the 777. From those experiences he has seen at first-hand the progress from analogue gauges to sophisticated glass cockpits. Like most pilots on the 777, Graeme loves the big twinjet.

One by one, the transatlantic flights have disappeared from the radar screens of Scottish controllers. The aircraft will be out of radar range for up to 4hr until they approach landfall over Newfoundland or Labrador. The radar controllers established safe separation between the flights at the start of the crossing. Now it is up to the oceanic controllers to maintain these separations. To do this, they rely on position reports filed by the flight crews at every 10° longitude.

This procedure has changed little since the birth of oceanic air traffic control. However, satellite-based navigation and communication are poised to revolutionise air traffic control, an advance hailed as the most significant development in the history of ATC since the introduction of radar.

World aviation organisations are looking at alternatives because they anticipate the current ATC system based on ground-based navigational aids, radar and voice communications will be increasingly hard-pressed to handle the increasing numbers of flights, expected to grow at 5% a year. Already in some parts of the world, the current ATC system is operating near capacity and the result is in-flight holds, gate holds and less than optimum altitude assignments.

On oceanic tracks, large separations are kept between aircraft because of the uncertainty of HF radio communications and the fact it is a non-radar environment. This ensures safety but it also makes for inefficient use of the airspace.

But a new ATC system called the Future Air Navigation System (FANS) is changing the way aircraft are handled on some routeings across the Pacific and the Far East. With FANS, pilots navigate using GPS and communicate with ATC through satcom or VHF datalinks. A FANS-equipped aircraft automatically transmits position reports as often as every 5min using signals from the GPS and transmitted to ATC via datalink. This information is used to generate graphic displays of oceanic flights, similar to the radar displays used by domestic controllers.

The goal is to reduce separation between oceanic flights from the current 100nm or more down to 50nm.

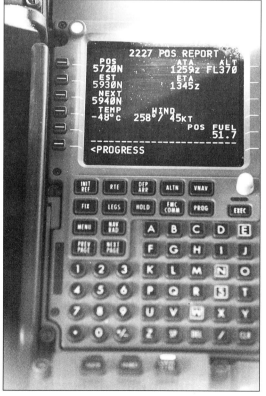

```
        2227 POS REPORT
 POS             ATA      ALT
5720N          1259z  FL370
 EST             ETA
5930N          1345z
 NEXT
5940N
 TEMP          WIND
-48°C      258°/45KT
                POS FUEL
                  51.7
--------------------------------
<PROGRESS
```

Additional system improvements could reduce that even further to 30nm and possibly to the separation standards used now in domestic airspace.

To have FANS capability, aircraft must be equipped for several functions: the ability to transmit position reports automatically to ATC; ATC datalink; GPS; and a flight planning tool called required time of arrival. This allows the pilots to assign a time constraint to a waypoint using the FMC. The computer then automatically adjusts the cruise speed to achieve that schedule within 30sec. The 777 has FANS-1 capability installed as basic equipment.

Above:
As the aircraft passes 5720N, Graeme files a position report with Shanwick using the high frequency radio.

Left
He refers to the FMC display for the flight's ETA to the next waypoint.

Opposite:
The ND range is set to 640nm and the route stretches ahead of the aircraft symbol. On the right side is the symbol marking BIKF, the airport at Keflavik, Iceland. Displayed in the upper left are the wind arrow, which gives the wind speed and direction, and the jet's groundspeed and true airspeed. In the upper right, it is noted that the next waypoint is 5930N, the midpoint of the ocean crossing, which is 215nm away and will be reached at 13.45Z.

The improvements of FANS-1 take air traffic control a step towards a concept called 'free flight'. This would give pilots the freedom of navigating direct to their destinations without assigned routeings. Speed or altitude would be restricted by ATC only in congested terminal airspace or to avoid potential conflicts. It has been described as the flexibility of VFR flight with the protection of IFR traffic separation.

As a glance at any IFR chart will reveal, the existing navigation system is based on a rigid system of airways linking ground-based navaids. Allowing aircraft to fly direct routeings at their most efficient altitudes and speeds would save airlines billions of dollars in time and fuel.

British Airways Flight 2227 is navigating using GPS but the remainder of these space-based improvements remain a few years off yet on Atlantic routes. And until then, the age-old tradition of HF radio reports remains the backbone of air traffic control. It is just before 13.00Z when Graeme dons his headset to file the position report passing 5720N.

First Officer R/T: 'Shanwick, Shanwick it's Speedbird Seven November, position.'

Shanwick R/T: 'Speedbird calling Shanwick, go ahead.'

First Officer R/T: 'Shanwick, Speedbird Seven November position, copy Gander, five seven north, two zero west, one two five niner, level three seven zero. Five niner north, three zero west, one three four six. Next five niner north, four zero west.'

In his report, Graeme has told the radio operator the aircraft callsign, their present position and time, flight level, the next position on the assigned route and the time they expect to get there and the waypoint following that one. Because control of the flight will pass to Gander at the next waypoint, Graeme has also asked Shanwick to copy Canadian controllers on the position report. At each reporting point, the crew also perform a series of checks to ensure the flight is on track. They confirm that the initial true track and distance to the next waypoint shown on the ND match the flightplan. They also make sure the aircraft turns to the new heading. In rare cases, a flight crew has forgotten to engage LNAV, leaving the autopilot on HDG mode instead. This means the aircraft is flying a set heading rather than the course programmed in the FMC. These errors have led to a loss of separation as the off-course aircraft wanders onto an adjacent track. The fuel burn and the FMC prediction of how much fuel will remain on landing are also checked against the flightplan for any discrepancies. For example, the flight may be using more fuel than expected due to stronger than forecast headwinds. That is not a problem today though. The jet has 51.7 tonnes of fuel in the tanks, comfortably above the 49.5 tonnes required at this point.

Passing 5930N at 13.45Z, the flight is half-way across the ocean and control now hands over to the Gander oceanic control centre. Graeme files his position reports to the radio operators at the Gander international flight service station who take the information and pass it on to the oceanic controllers. The flight continues to experience a 50kt headwind, resulting in a groundspeed of 449kt.

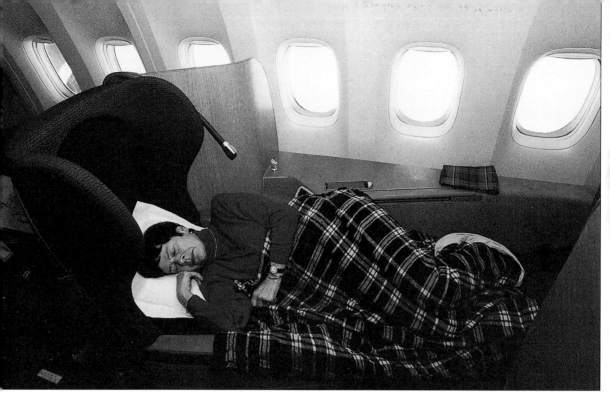

Top:
The luxurious first class seats recline flat, allowing a traveller to pass a flight in blissful sleep.

Above:
Passengers can choose from a variety of video and audio selections. In economy class, the screens
are built into the seatbacks.

By this point, passengers have long since settled into their routine for the flight. Some use the time to sleep, some recline in their seats and relax with a good book while other travellers, especially those in business class, pull out laptop computers to knock off a few hours' work.

Passengers also pass the time with the help of the 777's in-flight entertainment system. This sophisticated system provides a choice of eight channels of videos and a selection of CD-quality music that ranges from jazz and classical performances to British pop and country. Selections are made using a handset at each seat which also doubles as a telephone. The introduction of the entertainment system has not been without its share of problems, much to the frustration of passengers and crew alike. Most of the bugs have been worked out but it is still rare that a flight is completed without at least one complaint about the audio or video feed.

Left:
The large overhead bins retract into the ceiling, leaving plenty of headroom. This slick feature helps give the cabin a spacious feel.

Below:
A cabin management system allows the flight attendants to control the lighting, fine tune the temperature in each of the three cabins and check on the levels in the waste water and potable water tanks. The selections are made using a touch-sensitive screen.

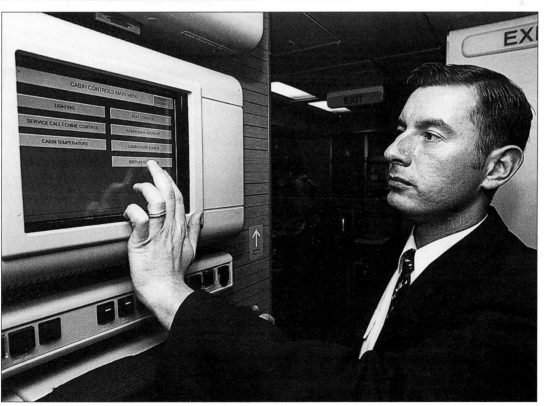

Above:
The Cabin Service Director makes his office at the front of the aircraft, just outside the flightdeck door. The tall stack of tape players are used to run the videos.

Boeing spent a lot of time on the design of the 777 cabin and the final product reflects that work. For starters, the fuselage cross-section of the 777 is perfectly round, a first for a Boeing jetliner. This makes for a large cabin which at 19ft 3in is wider than any other jetliner except for the 747. But Boeing also used clever design features to make the cabin appear spacious. The cabin is brighter, thanks to indirect lighting and bigger windows. Straighter cabin walls provide more shoulder room for passengers sitting in window seats. Large overhead stowage bins tuck away into the ceiling to give 6ft 4in of headroom over the centre row of seating. Boeing designed the cabin with what it calls flex zones. The plumbing and electrical fixtures in the cabin are built so the lavatories and galleys can be moved in 1in increments within these zones. This gives airlines the ability to change cabin configuration and seating arrangements in as little as 72hr, compared to two or three weeks on other aircraft.

Of course, the look and features of the jet's cabin are left to the airline's own designers. When it came time for British Airways to refurbish its first class cabin, it spared

little. The cabin on the airline's IGW models seats 14 in sumptuous comfort and for those who can afford it, this is the only way to fly. The seats are designed as private little nooks and can recline flat to become a 6ft 6in bed. With a pillow and blanket, it is the perfect arrangement for overnight flights. In the Club World cabin, British Airways' business class, 56 travellers are seated in a 2-3-2 arrangement. The seats are more like armchair recliners, each with its own reading light and video screen that comes out of the armrest. A generous 50in pitch provides plenty of legroom, which is vitally important to long-haul business travellers. Economy class is located at the rear of the jet and seats 197 in a 3-3-3 layout. Seats are comfortable and the video screens are conveniently located in the seatback ahead.

The airline's five base model 777s are configured to seat 235 passengers with almost two-thirds of the aircraft dedicated to first and business class seating. These aircraft are used primarily on lucrative Middle East routes. The IGW models used on US routes have a larger economy section and seat 267 passengers.

The cabin crew has been busy since the departure tending to the passengers and preparing and serving lunch from the three galleys. The selection for first class passengers reads like the menu from a fine restaurant. The choice of hors d'oeuvres included lobster and prawn salad, a fruit plate, or warm smoked salmon tart. Entrées included roasted loin of lamb, pan-fried sea bass, Moroccan-style grilled vegetable kebabs and Indian buttered chicken. For drinks, passengers had a choice of nine fine wines and a selection of spirits, liqueurs and beers.

Though well-versed in the art of customer service, a flight attendant's main duty is to ensure passenger safety. It is a role that unfortunately too many travellers take for granted. The job is a demanding one that requires long duty days. But it makes for an interesting lifestyle and the varied destinations can compensate for the long days flight attendants spend on their feet. Much like the pilots, each cabin crew member gets a rest break on a long flight like this. They usually spend this quiet time in a crew chair located to one side of the forward galley which has a curtain that can be drawn for some privacy.

The cabin is pressurised by compressed air taken from each engine, passed through air conditioning packs where it is cooled and then vented into the cabin. It may seem strange that the air has to be cooled first, given that the outside air temperature at this altitude is a frosty -65° Celsius. But the cabin air is drawn from the engines' high pressure compressors, just before the combustion chamber, and compression has made it extremely hot.

Opposite above:
Working from a galley no bigger than a small apartment kitchen, flight attendant Yvette Brooks prepares the fine food to be served in the first class cabin.

Opposite:
Flight attendants Nigel Tostevin and Clare Hardwick are ready to serve beverages to passengers in the Club World cabin.

This hot bleed air is also used to de-ice the engine cowlings and the leading edges of the wings. At this height, the cabin altitude is just over 6,000ft. The cabin pressure is controlled by two outflow valves which automatically open and close to change the rate that air leaves the aircraft.

Rehman returns to the flightdeck at 14.17Z and slips into the Captain's seat to stand in for Kevin. Eleven minutes later, the jet passes 5940N. It is a cloudless day and the view out the windows is magnificent, if not a bit forbidding. Passengers on the right side are treated to a great view of Greenland, less than 100nm to the north. The large island presents a daunting sight with its icy expanse and rocky cliffs. Out of sight some 400 miles up the west coast and just a bit inland is Sondrestrom, an airport occasionally nominated as a diversion airfield for ETOPS planning. The airfield is located at the head of a narrow, steep-sided fjord and although the setting is rather inhospitable, on a day with good weather it would suit the purpose just fine.

The view below is no more welcoming where large icebergs and floes of pack ice compete for space on the ocean surface.

The Atlantic was a formidable challenge for early fliers like John Alcock and Arthur Whitten Brown. Their 16hr flight in 1919 from Newfoundland to Ireland in a Vickers Vimy biplane bomber with its open cockpit was the first nonstop transatlantic crossing.

Charles Lindbergh made history with his New York to Paris flight in 1927 in a single-engine Ryan aircraft, christened the *Spirit of St Louis*. He was not first to cross the Atlantic but he was the first to do it alone. During his 33hr flight, he battled numbing fatigue and at times descended to just a few feet above the water to see the whitecaps and get a reading of the wind direction. 'It's a fierce, unfriendly sea — a sea that would batter the largest ocean liner. I feel naked above it, as though stripped of all protection, conscious of the terrific strength of the waves, of the thinness of cloth on my wings, the turbulence of the storm clouds,' he wrote in his book *The Spirit of St Louis*.

'Paris is over a thousand miles away! And there's still a continent to find. I must be prepared to strike a fog-covered European coast hundreds of miles off course; and, if necessary, to fly above clouds all the hours of another night. How can I pass through such ordeals if I can't wake my mind and stir my body?…Can I complete this flight to Paris? Can I even reach Irish coast?'

In just a generation the trip across the Atlantic has become much easier. Today, jets transport passengers high above the weather in a comfortable pressurised cabin where they can watch a film, enjoy a drink, listen to a selection of music or get some work done on a laptop computer. And yet these large expanses of water continue to present a unique challenge for some commercial jets. Just over a decade ago, twin-engine operations across the North Atlantic were virtually non-existent. The introduction of twinjets like the Airbus A300 and Boeing 767 and 757 in the mid-1980s convinced regulatory authorities to permit twins on routes 1-3hr from an airport but only after an aircraft type had demonstrated its reliability and the airline met stringent equipment and training requirements.

The new rules changed the way people are flying. In the late 1970s, 85% of the flights across the Atlantic were

Above:
A forbidding view of ocean and ice. From the earliest days of flight, the oceans have presented a unique challenge to aviators. Even today, commercial twinjets are allowed to fly long over-water legs only after proving their reliability on thousands of shorter flights.

in 747s. Now it is about 30%. By using the smaller twins, airlines are able to offer direct flights on thinner markets. These new services save passengers the headache of having to travel first to a hub like New York, Chicago or London to catch an overseas flight. The result is shorter travel times and more nonstop services to a greater number of cities.

Today, the reliability of modern jet engines has made such flights routine. But until the 777, a twin-engined jet was granted approval to fly long, over-water legs only after it had built a track record over several years and several hundred thousand hours on shorter flights. Until the approval was met, flights were restricted to routes within 60min flying time of an airport at the single engine cruising speed. On paper, it was possible to cross the Atlantic but the dogleg routeing required by such a restriction would hardly be practical for commercial operations.

Boeing, though, set the ambitious goal of ensuring the 777 had approval to fly 180min ETOPS routes — up to 3hr or about 1,200nm from an airport — on its first day in revenue service. It was a remarkable challenge for the manufacturer, especially since the 777 was a new aircraft using new engines. Yet Boeing had to offer instant ETOPS to compete with the three- and four-engined jets offered by competing aircraft manufacturers.

To do it, Boeing embarked on a flight test programme unprecedented in the company's long history. The programme involved nine 777s in all — six devoted to the type certification of the airframe and the Pratt & Whitney, Rolls-Royce and General Electric engines. Another three aircraft each flew 1,000 flights ranging from 1hr to more than 9hr to demonstrate the reliability for early ETOPS approvals of each of the three engine-airframe combinations.

Components of the aircraft were 'flown' on the ground as well as in Boeing's Integrated Aircraft Systems Laboratory, a $360 million centre also known as 'airplane zero'. This Seattle facility is where aircraft components were tested individually and then together as they would be working on the actual plane. For example, the 777's flight control system, including its fly-by-wire technology and parts of the electrical and hydraulic systems, were tested together on the flight controls test rig. This enabled design staff to uncover and correct potential problems not usually detected until the flight tests.

At the heart of ETOPS approval is engine reliability and the GE90 engines which power the 777s operated by British Airways were subjected to a rigorous certification process involving 13 engines and more than 19,000 cycles in ground and flight testing.

The GE90 is the world's biggest engine and its large fan produces a high bypass ratio of nine to one. That means for every part of air that enters the engine core, nine parts pass through the fan blades and around the core. Accelerated by the front fan and the shape of the engine nacelle, this bypass air provides a significant portion of the total thrust. It is also a key factor in making the engine the quietest of those on the 777. British Airways uses the GE90-85B, which produces 84,700lb, to power its heavier IGW models. A higher thrust model of the engine — the GE90-92B — was

Left:
Acting on the input of one airline concerned the jet's 199ft wingspan would be too big for airport gates designed for DC-10s and L-1011s, Boeing designed a folding wing option. By 1998, no airline had ordered the option.

Below
Passengers should not worry when they see the 777's wings flex up and down in flight — in one test of the airframe's strength, Boeing pulled the wings of a test 777 fuselage 24ft above their normal position before they broke. *Boeing*

Above:
The 777 was put through the toughest flight test programme ever devised by Boeing. Here a flight crew purposely over-rotate on take-off, dragging the tail along the runway. This dramatic performance test was used to determine take-off speeds for the aircraft. *Boeing*

Inset:
Visually, the increased gross weight model of the 777 is indistinguishable from the base model. It has a higher maximum take-off weight of up to 286,900kg and can carry 45,220gal of fuel — 14,220gal more than the base model, giving it the range to fly 5,960nm to 7,230nm. *John M. Dibbs*

certified by the FAA in July 1996, at 92,000lb of thrust, the most powerful engine ever certified by the agency. GE had also started work on the GE90-100B — a 100,000lb thrust engine — but the project was put on hold to await more favourable market conditions.

The first GE90-powered 777 had its maiden flight on 2 February 1995. Problems in testing delayed certification and pushed back the scheduled delivery to British Airways by two months to November 1995. The GE90-76B — an 84,700lb thrust engine derated to 76,400lb — entered revenue service with the airline that same month on routes from London to destinations throughout the Middle East including Dubai, Muscat

and Jeddah. The engine was granted regulatory approval by the FAA for 180min ETOPS flights in October 1996. The Joint Airworthiness Authorities (JAA), the European regulatory body, was more conservative and granted approval only for 120min ETOPS flights. British Airways got approval to extend this to 138min and immediately started 777 flights between London and Boston. This odd number is common in ETOPS planning for it allows an airline to plan a transatlantic routeing based on alternative airports in the Canadian Maritimes and British Isles. Anything less than 138min and a flight must include the Azores or Iceland as mid-ocean alternatives. The JAA granted the GE-powered 777 full 180min ETOPS approval in October 1997.

By March 1998, the more than 90 GE90s in commercial service had logged 205,038hr with an in-flight shutdown rate of 0.006 per 1,000hr and a dispatch rate of 99.93%. The average engine had 2,186hr and was logging 8.92hr a day.

The GE90 has had its teething pains. British Airways suffered one in-flight shutdown when a problem with a fuel controller caused the engine to run down. British Airways staff praise its reliability as good for a new engine but say airline maintenance staff have been kept busy performing more checks on the GE90s than were expected. In April 1997, the FAA issued an emergency airworthiness directive requiring inspections for faulty ball-bearings on the engines. The AD followed ball-bearing failures on two British Airways aircraft though neither failure resulted in an engine shutdown. As a precaution, British Airways switched the three IGW aircraft it had at the time off transatlantic routes and onto European and Middle East flights while engineers probed the problem. The ball-bearings are installed in the gearbox which drives the engine accessories providing back-up electrical power. More recently, a British Airways 777 suffered an engine failure while departing from Heathrow in March 1998. The aircraft, bound for Boston, had just started its take-off roll when there was a failure within the low pressure turbine of a GE90-85B. The failure was contained and there was no fire although the engine was damaged. The problem was traced to misassembly during manufacture.

An ETOPS flight has many operational considerations starting with the pre-flight planning. The dispatcher establishes the optimum route and then selects the en route alternatives based on the weather forecasts. As noted, the planned ETOPS diversionary airports on this flight are Manchester and Goose Bay but at points over the ocean other airports like Shannon or Keflavik, Iceland, are much closer. In deciding where to land the flight crew would consider how serious the emergency is and how fast they need to get the jet on the ground, what maintenance facilities are at the field and the inconvenience to passengers. If the situation allowed, a crew's first choice would be an airport served by British Airways. This would mean the presence of maintenance staff and an easier time getting travellers on another flight to their destination.

Above:
Powering British Airways' fleet of 777s is the GE90, the largest commercial jet engine ever made. The GE90-85B used on the IGW models produces 84,700lb of thrust. The thrust of a single 777 engine alone easily exceeds all four Pratt & Whitney JT3C-6 engines on the 707. A change in the electronic engine control is all that is required to increase the thrust to 90,000lb.

Below:
Boeing's first 777 in flight. *Boeing*

A key factor in diversion planning is the equal time point which on this flight was just west of 30° West and passed at 14.04Z. Before that position it would have been quicker to divert back to Manchester. Now the alternative of Goose Bay is closer with every passing minute and if a diversion is required the crew will complete the ocean crossing and land there.

Should an emergency require a descent, the aircraft would first be turned 90° off the oceanic track to avoid conflicting with traffic below. In addition to requesting clearance from oceanic control, the crew would broadcast their intentions on 121.5MHz to let nearby aircraft know what was going on. The flight would then take up a course 30nm north or south of the oceanic track and parallel to it. If the aircraft was diverting to an airport south or north of its current position, such as Keflavik, the crew would descend below FL290. This would take them out of North Atlantic track airspace where it would be safe to turn to the diversionary airfield without risk of conflicting with jets on other tracks. The diversions page of the FMC makes decisions easier. It gives the crew a list of the four closest diversionary airports, the time it would take to fly to each one and the fuel remaining after the diversion was completed. The pilot can select an airport and start the diversion with just a few keystrokes.

Although much of the ETOPS requirements centre on engine reliability, a loss of pressurisation can cause just as much trouble as an engine fire or failure. That is because a pressurisation problem could force a descent to 15,000ft where at heavier weights, fuel burn jumps to 5,288kg per engine per hour, almost twice the consumption at normal cruising altitudes. When airline dispatchers decide the fuel load and select alternative airfields, they plan for the worst case scenario — an engine failure and pressurisation problem that forces a single-engine diversion at 15,000ft. A single engine operating at maximum continuous power consumes 6,927kg an hour at 15,000ft. That is more than both engines burn cruising at normal altitudes.

Another concern flying so far from land is fire. The fire suppression system for the cargo compartment is designed to handle a fire at the worst possible time — when the jet could be 3hr from an airport. The forward, aft and bulk cargo compartments are all equipped with smoke detectors. In the event of a fire warning for one of the compartments, the crew would first arm the extinguishing system to discharge in the appropriate compartment. Next they would press the discharge switch. This would immediately release halon from two bottles and start a timer for the slow, metered release of another three bottles over the next 180min to keep the fire under control during the time it took to divert.

The engines themselves are protected by two halon bottles. To extinguish an engine fire, the crew would switch off the autothrottle for the engine, close the thrust lever, select the fuel control switch to CUTOFF and then pull the fire switch for that engine. This arms both fire bottles, closes the fuel valves to halt the flow of fuel to the engine, trips off the engine's electrical generators, stops the flow of hydraulic fluid and shuts off the engine-driven hydraulic pump, and closes the engine bleed air valves. Turning the fire handle breaks the seal on one bottle, releasing halon to the selected engine. If the fire warning remains after 30sec, the handle is turned the other way to discharge the second bottle into the engine.

At 15.16Z, the flight passes 5750N. The jet has consumed just less than half its fuel load, leaving 36.2 tonnes in the tanks. Each engine is now burning three tonnes an hour. The next waypoint is LOACH, the end of the ocean crossing. It is 250nm away and should be reached at 15.51Z.

Below:
Pilots new to the big twinjet learn their craft in one of two 777 simulators operated by British Airways at its training centre next to Heathrow Airport.

Bottom:
Captain Nick Feakes, the 777 training manager, is pictured in one of the simulators. With about 16 pilots for each 777 in the fleet, the sophisticated machines are kept busy with initial and recurrent training.

The quiet of cruise stands in stark contrast to the orchestrated mayhem the pilots face during their twice yearly visits to the simulator. There they face every manner of emergency — engine failure on take-off, windshear, fires, decompression and single-engine approaches to a runway masked by rain and fog. It is all hard flying, with more things going wrong on a simulated flight than they will encounter in a lifetime of flying. The instrument rating renewal, for example, usually hits the pilot with an engine failure on take-off and then requires him to fly the aircraft manually in instrument conditions on a short flight and shoot a single-engine approach down to minimums.

The recurrent training is done in two 4hr sessions over two days. The first day is the actual check ride to maintain the rating and the second day is the refresher. In addition to the usual offerings of engine fires and failures, pilots are given more complicated emergencies to test crew interaction. One scenario is an engine failure over the North Atlantic which forces a diversion. Another is getting a bomb threat in flight. The trainers want to see the crew manage the emergency to a successful outcome but are also looking at how they work together to solve complex problems. In a tribute to the reliability of today's aircraft, most flights are routine but crews can still face circumstances that take them

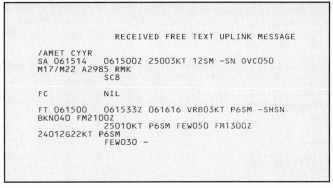

RECEIVED FREE TEXT UPLINK MESSAGE

/AMET CYYR
SA 061514   061500Z 25003KT 12SM -SN OVC050
M17/M22 A2985 RMK
             SC8

FC   NIL

FT 061500   061533Z 061616 VRB03KT P6SM -SHSN
BKN040 FM2100Z
             25010KT P6SM FEW050 FM1300Z
24012G22KT P6SM
             FEW030 -

Left:
Should a diversion be necessary en route, the alternate page of the FMC helps with the decision-making. AT 15.43Z, near the end of the ocean crossing, the FMC displays four alternate possibilities — Goose Bay (CYYR), Gander (CYQX), St John's (CYYT), all in Newfoundland and Sondrestrom, Greenland (BGSF). Also shown is the ETA to each airport and the forecast fuel that would be remaining after the diversion.

Above:
Goose Bay, an ETOPS alternate airport, continues to have good weather with just light snow showers reported.

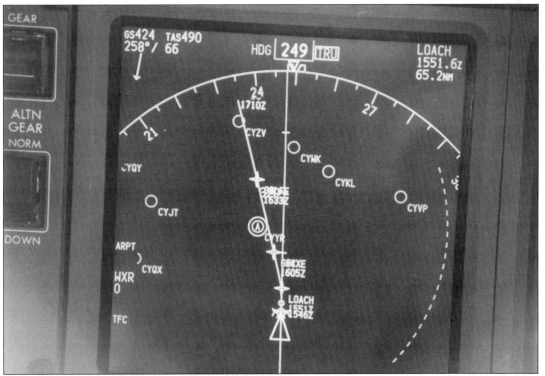

Above:
The jet is just 65nm from LOACH and the end of the ocean crossing. A brisk headwind blowing directly on the nose slows the flight to a groundspeed of 424kt.

The jet has climbed to 39,000ft and is maintaining its cruise speed of Mach 0.84. The next waypoint is Rivière du Loup. The small circles on the ND represent airports.

away from their pre-planned routeing. Bad weather, ATC delays or mechanical problems can all force a crew to put an alternative plan into action. It is in situations like these that cockpit resource management — the skill of working together — is put to good use.

For pilots moving on to the 777, the first stop is groundschool. Each day, they will spend 4hr using an interactive computer terminal to learn the aircraft systems and then it is off to the simulator for 2hr of practical work to reinforce the normal and abnormal systems procedures. Once ground school is done, the pilots spend a further 36hr in one of two full-motion 777 simulators owned by British Airways.

At the end of the training, the new pilot flies 14 sectors under the supervision of a training captain. Pilots new to the 777 are usually impressed by the relative simplicity of the jet, especially those transitioning from the 747 Classic with its steamship-style gauges and long checklists.

Introducing and supporting an aircraft in service requires much organisation and planning. The management team is headed by the 777 chief pilot, who also looks after the 747-100 and Concorde fleets. He is assisted by a technical team and a training team. With the airline taking delivery of one new 777 a month, it is

an especially busy time for Captain Nick Feakes, the 777 training manager, and his cadre of 40 training and check captains. The airline averages about eight crews for each 777 and in the winter of 1998 had about 260 777 pilots working the line. Not only does his department have to provide initial training to all these pilots but annual recurrent training as well.

Kevin has returned to the flightdeck. During his break, he had some lunch and made the rounds of the cabin to chat with passengers, a luxury not possible on flights with only two pilots.

At 15.46Z, the oceanic controller requests the flight call Moncton Centre 5min from LOACH. At the proper time, Graeme switches to the VHF frequency and makes the call.

First Officer R/T: 'Moncton, it's Speedbird Seven November.'

Moncton Centre: 'Speedbird Seven November, squawk code zero seven four six.'

First Officer R/T: 'Roger, code zero seven four six and Moncton, any chance of flight level three niner zero?'

Moncton Centre: 'Speedbird Seven November, cleared direct Rivière du Loup and up to flight level three niner zero.'

The controller has cleared the flight to its requested altitude and direct to a small Quebec town on the south shore of the St Lawrence River. The aircraft passes

Above:
Kevin has the North Atlantic map clipped just
below the window. Next to it is a copy of the
flightplan which he uses to track the flight's
progress.

Below:
Rehman takes over in the right seat while
Graeme goes to the cabin for his rest period.

Opposite above:
The Green Mountains of Vermont are a summer and winter playground. Here downhill ski trails are visible on the tree-clad slopes.

Opposite below:
The flight passes abeam Stewart International Airport, a former military field located at Newburgh, New York, in the Hudson Valley about 50nm north of New York City.

Right:
The centre console does double duty as an informal table for the crew's late afternoon snack.

LOACH at 15.50Z to end the ocean crossing, 3hr 40min after it started. Power increases to 101.7% N1 for the short climb to the new altitude and fuel burn rises to 4.2 tonnes per engine per hour. The heading indicators are selected back to magnetic. Atlanta is still another 1,781nm away.

Aircraft exiting oceanic airspace must be returned to 2,000ft vertical separations before mixing with domestic traffic. To accommodate this, a transition area extends about an hour's flying time west of 50° West where controllers can sort out cruising heights before the flights join the high altitude airways. It will take 90min to fly the 659nm to Rivière du Loup. This long stretch is passed with a constant stream of visitors to the flightdeck. Unlike stringent FAA regulations which require American pilots to do their work behind closed doors, the British Airways crew has an open door policy. They happily describe the jet's workings to curious passengers, possibly inspiring one or two future pilots among the children who have wandered up front. The visitors are as varied as a Royal Air Force test pilot and a 5-year-old boy who asks 'What do those do?' and points at the throttles. 'Those make the plane go faster and slower,' Graeme explains.

Rivière du Loup is reached at 17.21Z. The aircraft has been crabbing to the right, flying a heading of 240° to make good a track of 231° against the wind blowing from the northwest at 70kt.

The TCAS system displays the positions of two aircraft flying ahead. Sure enough, looking out the front windows, the jets can be seen trailing contrails across the blue sky. Passing overhead Rivière du Loup, the 777 banks slightly to the left to take up a new heading for the 341nm-leg to Albany, the capital of New York state. Stretching off to the southwest is the St Lawrence River, the major commercial waterway that links the Great Lakes with the Atlantic Ocean and provides shipping access to the heartland of North America.

Kevin picks out the jet's routeing on a high-altitude aviation chart and compares it to the Captain's Atlas resting on his lap. The aviation chart is obviously needed to navigate in the sky but beyond its depiction of airways, VORs and airports, it gives no hint of the scenery below. The Captain's Atlas is the best of both worlds — it has the airways overlaid on a road map, showing the location of cities, rivers and highways, which makes it an invaluable aid for pointing out landmarks to passengers. For the rest of the route, the flight will parallel the Appalachian Mountains, the second largest mountain system in North America. The Appalachians stretch about 1,500 miles between the Gaspe Peninsula in Quebec and central Alabama in the southern US. The mountain range gives passengers plenty of attractive scenery to look at. The Green

Mountains, as the Appalachians are known in Vermont, pass on the right side. Lake Champlain is visible a little further to the west. The airports in Rochester and Syracuse in upper New York State and the New York area airports of LaGuardia, JFK and Newark appear as blue circles on the ND.

At 17.57Z, the flight checks in with Boston Centre. The actual city of Boston is less than 150nm to the east.

First Officer R/T: 'Boston Centre, good afternoon, it's Speedbird Seven November level three niner zero.'

Boston Centre: 'Speedbird Seven November, roger.'

```
        RECEIVED FREE TEXT UPLINK MESSAGE

/AMET KATL
SA 061400    061353Z 33010KT 10SM FEW015 BKN250
01/M03 A2987
          RMK A02

FC        NIL

FT 061132    061120Z 061212 32014G20KT P6SM
OVC015 FM1500
          31012KT P6SM OVC015 TEMPO 1518
OVC022 FM1900
          30010KT P6SM OVC025 TEMPO 2024
SCT025 BKN035
          FM0100 32008KT P6SM OVC020 PROB30
0612 5SM -RA SN
          OVC015 -
```

On the ramp back at Gatwick, the crew entered a number known as the cost index into the FMC to tell it whether the emphasis should be on speed or efficiency. The FMC then uses this factor in its calculations at every stage of the flight — climbs, its suggestion of optimum cruising altitudes and descents. For this trip, the pilots used a cost index of 100, a selection commonly used for most flights which strikes a balance between speed and fuel

economy. Now with the aircraft well ahead of schedule, Kevin changes the cost index to zero. This is the maximum range factor and will cause the aircraft to slow to a more economical speed of about Mach 0.83. This change will save several hundred kilograms of fuel while costing only a few minutes' extra time en route.

With the arrival now less than 2hr away, Kevin turns his attention to the Atlanta approach plates and sorts

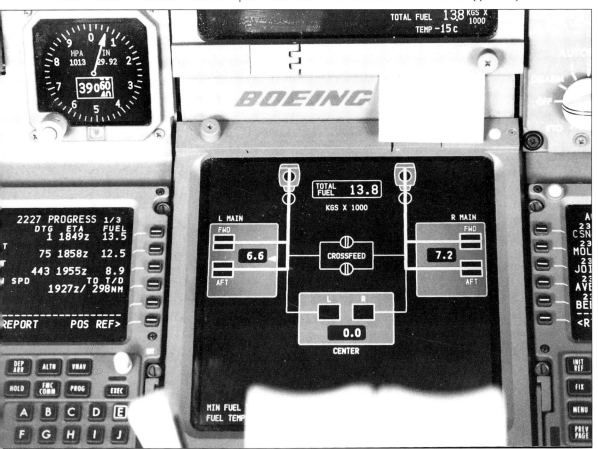

Opposite above:
The weather in Atlanta remains good.

Opposite below:
The fuel synoptic shows 13.8 tonnes of fuel remaining in the two main tanks.

This page
**As the end of cruise draws near, Atlanta approach plates and airport diagrams
are pulled out for review.**

through the STARs to pick out the likely routeing into Atlanta.

At most major airports, aircraft are guided by radar to intercept the instrument landing system for a particular runway. The ILS consists of two elements: the localiser guides an aircraft onto the extended centreline of the runway and tells the pilots when they are left, right or directly on course. A separate glidepath transmitter emits a beam to guide aircraft on a smooth descent to the runway, usually at about 700-900 fpm. The ILS signals are picked up by multiple receivers on the aircraft and displayed by two bars on the PFDs, one representing the glideslope and the other the localiser. Flying a successful ILS approach means keeping the bars centred in the middle of the display, something easier said than done on a rainy night with a crosswind gusting at 25kt.

The ILS is the most precise of all approach aids and is divided into three categories. Category I allows approaches down to a minimum altitude of 200ft above the ground with a visibility on the runway of 1,800ft. Category II approach limits are a 100ft ceiling and a visibility of 1,200ft. Category III approaches are used in conditions of the poorest visibility and for a 'no decision height operation', there is no requirement for the pilot to see the runway or approach lights prior to touchdown. British Airways requires a minimum runway visibility of about 250ft. This is more to facilitate taxiing than the landing itself.

In such bad weather, pilots would fly an autoland approach. During an automatic approach, the autopilot guides the aircraft down the ILS with the autothrottle maintaining the desired speed. Below 1,500ft above ground, flare and rollout modes arm and 'LAND 3' appears on the PFD if all three autopilot channels are serviceable. The handling pilot will guard the controls during the approach right to the end of the landing roll, ready to take over if necessary. During the early stages of the approach, the autopilots will crab the jet to correct for a crosswind. When just a few hundred feet above the ground, the autopilots straighten the nose for landing and drop a wing to remain aligned with the centreline. At 50ft, the jet flares, the autothrottle retards power to idle and it touches down smoothly. The brakes apply automatically, the autopilot lowers the nosewheel to the runway and uses rudder and nosewheel steering to stay on the centreline — all without the touch of a human hand.

To do an automatic landing on a bright sunny day is one thing. Flying it while enveloped in cloud as the jet descends to an unseen runway is quite another. In thick fog, the crew may catch a glimpse of the pavement only as the wheels touch. And then the challenge is to find the terminal building! The 777 is also certified for a single-engine autoland and the simulator provides a dramatic display of the system's capabilities. If an engine fails on the approach, the autopilots use the appropriate amount of rudder trim to counter the resulting yaw, increase power on the remaining engine to stay on the ILS and continue the approach to a safe landing. The electrical system automatically reconfigures to compensate for the lost generator on the failed engine. 'LAND 3' remains displayed on the PFDs indicating the autopilots remain safely in control. The toughest job for a pilot is to sit on his hands and not take any unwarranted action.

During the 777 conversion course, 4hr are dedicated to low-visibility approaches in the simulator. The trainees will also shoot several autolands on the line which clears them to fly approaches to the lowest weather minimums.

At 18.20Z, Boston Centre clears the flight to the Pottstown VOR, which is west of Philadelphia. The VOR is 77nm and about 10min flying time away from the jet's present position. The flight passes abeam New York and the skyscrapers of Manhattan are visible in the distance before a haze of high cloud slides below to obscure the fine view the crew and passengers have been enjoying since the end of the ocean crossing.

There has been a steady change of frequencies for the last half hour and now New York Centre calls with new instructions.

New York Centre: 'Speedbird Seven November Heavy, cleared direct to Casanova to join J48.'

The Casanova VOR is southwest of Washington, DC and from there the flight will join the high-altitude airway J48. The 'heavy' reference added to the callsign denotes the flight as a large aircraft which leaves in its wake a trail of disturbed air and turbulent eddies powerful enough to upset a smaller aircraft.

Special ATC rules are in place at airports when small and large aircraft are flying in closer proximity and the danger of a wake turbulence encounter is greater. Controllers allow extra space when sequencing a lighter aircraft behind a heavy jet on approach. They will also delay a take-off clearance for a lighter aircraft if the preceding aircraft was a large aircraft jet to allow time for the turbulence to dissipate.

With the ND range set to 640nm, Atlanta now appears at the top of the screen. The FMC is showing an arrival time of 19.56Z with 8.9 tonnes of fuel left in the tanks upon landing.

The flight is handed off to Washington Centre. It passes abeam Philadelphia and then directly overhead Washington's Dulles Airport, which is hidden by cloud. The jet continues over Virginia and unseen below on the left side is the magnificent Chesapeake Bay which opens out on to the Atlantic Ocean.

At 19.07Z, Graeme returns from his rest period and resumes his position in the right seat. The flightdeck is tidied up in preparation for landing. En route charts are stowed away, paperwork is filed or thrown out. A plastic bag looped over the armrest of Graeme's chair is the dumping ground for many of the bits of paper the crew have accumulated during the flight. The rapidly filling bag is a testament that the day of the paperless plane remains a few years off yet. With those chores complete, the crew indulge in one last treat — afternoon scones. Flight attendant Yvette Brooks brings forward a tray of warm scones with strawberry preserves and clotted cream. A British treat in the Deep South.

Arrival

Atlanta. It conjures up images of the grand old south, stately antebellum homes and Southern hospitality. Set in northern Georgia in the foothills of the Blue Ridge Mountains, this is a city with a colourful history. It served as a strategic Confederate supply depot during the Civil War before it was captured in 1864 by Union troops who burned it to the ground, an action popularised in the film *Gone With the Wind*. It was also the birthplace of civil rights leader Martin Luther King Jr.

It was also here in 1886 that a now famous fizzy drink was invented — Coca-Cola. Today, Atlanta is home to the world headquarters of the soft drink maker and the Cable News Network, better known to millions of television viewers as CNN. The city played host to the world in 1996 when it staged the summer Olympic Games.

This metropolitan area of 3 million people has evolved into a cosmopolitan business centre but reminders of its southern roots are everywhere — 40-odd streets in the city are named Peachtree.

Aviation buffs will also know it as home to ATL, aviation lingo for Hartsfield Atlanta International Airport. It is the second busiest airport in the United States and the world and one of the busiest transfer hubs anywhere, prompting the saying 'Whether you're going to heaven or hell, you still have to change planes in Atlanta.'

The airport's statistics are impressive. In 1997, Hartsfield handled 68.2 million passengers, second only to Chicago's O'Hare Airport and up 7.7% from the previous year. Heathrow ranked fifth at 57.9 million travellers. That same year, Hartsfield ranked third in aircraft movements with 794,621 take-offs and landings, averaging an impressive 2,100 flights a day.

Hartsfield is served by 18 domestic carriers and 15 foreign airlines and by 2005 passenger traffic at Atlanta is forecast to top 90 million a year with flights growing to 1.2 million.

Hartsfield is set on 3,750 acres of land south of the city's downtown core. It has four runways, two on the north side of the terminal complex and two to the south, all laid out on an east-west orientation.

The outer runways are devoted to arrivals and are capable of all-weather landings to Cat IIIb limits of a 600ft visibility. However, Runway 9 Right is certified for operations down to a 300ft runway visibility, one of five runways in the US with such low limits.

The layout enables air traffic control to treat each pair of runways as a separate airport. Separate ground and tower controllers are dedicated for each side of the operation, along with separate arrival and departure controllers. Traffic flows are organised so that departures for the south and east use the south runways and north and westbound departures use the north side. Arrivals are organised in similar fashion.

Aircraft park at five separate mid-field concourses, each almost a kilometre long, that have a total of 142 domestic and 24 international gates. These concourses are linked to each other and the main terminal building with its ticketing and check-in desks by a 3.5-mile underground automated people mover train. The newest concourse, Concourse E, opened in 1994 at a cost of $300 million to serve the growing number of international flights which are up by 10% over the last two years.

The radio chatter has picked up, giving a hint that the arrival is not far off. The frequency for Atlanta ATIS is tuned so the crew can find out the current weather and airport operating information.

Atlanta ATIS: 'Atlanta airport arrival information Bravo, one eight five three zulu. Wind variable at three, visibility one zero, ceiling two five thousand overcast, temperature seven, dewpoint one, altimeter two niner eight three. Simultaneous approaches are in progress. Visual approach two six right, visual approach two seven left. Notices to airmen, taxiway Mike closed between taxiway Lima three and taxiway Mike ten. Advise on initial contact that you information Bravo.'

Below:
Just prior to descent, Kevin conducts the approach briefing to review key details of the descent and landing.

(W.B. HARTSFIELD) **ATLANTA**
(MACEY,MACEY2) MACEY TWO **STAR**

| Trans alt **18000** | Trans lev **ATC** |

| **H2** | **ZH** |
| EFF 05 DEC 96 |

1. Expect radar vectors to final approach course after LOGEN.

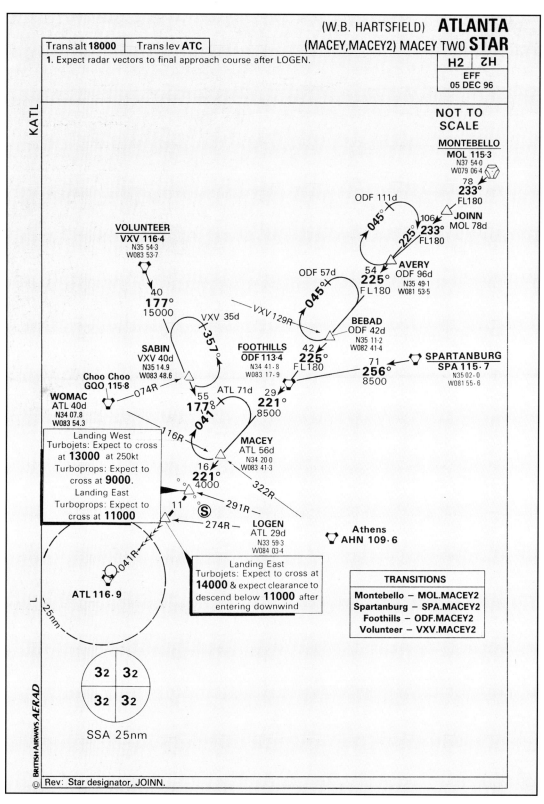

NOT TO SCALE

MONTEBELLO
MOL 115·3
N37 54·0
W079 06·4
78
233°
FL180

ODF 111d
045°
225°
233°
FL180
JOINN
MOL 78d
106

VOLUNTEER
VXV 116·4
N35 54·3
W083 53·7

54
225°
FL180
AVERY
ODF 96d
N35 49·1
W081 53·5

ODF 57d
045°

40
177°
15000

VXV 35d
VXV 129R

SABIN
VXV 40d
N35 14.9
W083 48.6

357°

FOOTHILLS
ODF 113·4
N34 41·8
W083 17·9

42
225°
FL180

BEBAD
ODF 42d
N35 11·2
W082 41·4

71
256°
8500

SPARTANBURG
SPA 115·7
N35 02·0
W081 55·6

Choo Choo
GQO 115·8
074R

55
177°
041°

ATL 71d
29
221°
8500

WOMAC
ATL 40d
N34 07.8
W083 54.3

116R

Landing West
Turbojets: Expect to cross at **13000** at 250kt
Turboprops: Expect to cross at **9000**.
Landing East
Turboprops: Expect to cross at **11000**

MACEY
ATL 56d
N34 20·0
W083 41·3

16
221°
4000

322R

291R

11

(S)

274R

LOGEN
ATL 29d
N33 59·3
W084 03·4

Athens
AHN 109·6

041R

ATL 116·9

25nm

Landing East
Turbojets: Expect to cross at **14000** & expect clearance to descend below **11000** after entering downwind

| **TRANSITIONS** |
| Montebello – MOL.MACEY2 |
| Spartanburg – SPA.MACEY2 |
| Foothills – ODF.MACEY2 |
| Volunteer – VXV.MACEY2 |

| 3₂ | 3₂ |
| 3₂ | 3₂ |

SSA 25nm

Rev: Star designator, JOINN.

Ten minutes before the top of descent, Kevin conducts the approach briefing and the items to be covered include safety altitudes, weather, runway condition and radio aids. Arriving from the northeast, the crew can expect the Macey Two STAR, one of four STARs used to funnel arrivals into Atlanta airport. The Macey Two routeing actually starts just over 350nm northeast of Hartsfield airport at the Montebello VOR, located north of Lynchburg, Virginia, which the flight passed about 20 minutes ago. The routeing takes the jet across North Carolina, passing west of Greensboro, and then into Georgia on a southwest course to Atlanta. Kevin starts the briefing by reviewing the altitude and speed restrictions of the STAR.

Captain: 'The first of the constraints, landing west turbojets are expected to cross WOMAC at 13,000 at 250 knots and that's been put into the FMC. Then on to LOGEN and the routeing takes us toward the Atlanta airport, expecting to be picked off for radar vectors onto one of the westerly runways, either two seven left or two six right are the likely options.'

The briefing continues as Kevin talks through the ILS approach to Runway 27 Left, highlighting the inbound heading of 272° to track the localiser, passing the outer marker at 2,800ft and a decision height of 1,200ft above sea level, 200ft above the field. This altitude, which is dialled up for display on the PFD for easy reference, marks the lowest altitude an aircraft can descend to during an instrument approach without seeing the ground. To continue at that point, the crew must see the runway or approach lights and be in position to make a safe landing. If not, they must abort the approach and go-around. With the arrival runway programmed into the FMC, it automatically tunes the ILS and shows the identifier on the PFDs. The jet's weight for landing is expected to be 192.5 tonnes, giving an approach speed, known as Vref, of 133kt. The higher the weight, the higher this speed and the longer the landing rollout.

Captain: 'There's nothing wrong with the aircraft that would affect the arrival, no significant weather and latest weather shows overcast skies with a light northwesterly breeze.'

The autobrake is set at 2 to give moderate braking on rollout which should stop the jet in about 6,000ft. Selecting maximum auto braking, typically reserved for emergencies, would shorten the landing roll to 3,700ft but the hard stop would be very uncomfortable for passengers. Kevin also tells Graeme he would like full reverse thrust applied after landing. Next he reviews the go-around procedure.

Captain: 'The go-around is ahead to fourteen hundred feet, 400 feet above the field, then left onto Atlanta VOR radial one eight zero to SCARR which is a waypoint to the south at 15 DME at 3,500 feet to hold. The person flying the aircraft in the event of a go-around will press the TO/GA button, say "go-around, flaps 20" and ensure the power comes up and that the autopilot follows the flight director or we manually follow the flight director. We'll clean up on schedule and level off at three and a half thousand feet.'

Opposite:
The chart showing the Macey Two arrival routeing into Atlanta. *Racal Avionics*

Above:
On the Arrivals page of the FMC, Kevin selects the STAR and expected ILS approach. The computer automatically tunes the required radio aids.

A go-around can be initiated for any number of reasons. The controller can ask a flight to go-around even after a landing clearance has been issued if, for example, the aircraft landing ahead is slow exiting the runway. Pilots can decide to go-around if they do not like the way the approach is proceeding. British Airways' rules require a go-around if at 500ft the aircraft is not stable in the landing configuration, speedbrakes are deployed, normal power is not set or speed is more than 20kt above the target threshold speed.

In the event of a go-around, the handling pilot calls 'Go around, flaps 20' to immediately remove the heavy drag of the landing flap. At the same time, the pilot will push the TO/GA buttons to initiate the manoeuvre. At the first push of the buttons, engine thrust will increase to give a 2,000fpm climb — more than adequate for most go-arounds. A second push of the buttons commands full power. Pushing the TO/GA buttons also commands the flight director to show the proper pitch attitude required for a climb or in the case of an automatic approach, commands the autopilot to fly the procedure.

Despite their mammoth size, the engines are surprisingly responsive. Certification rules require the engine to go from approach idle to 90% N1 in 8sec. The GE90 does it in 6.5sec and the aircraft wastes no time reversing its descent; during automatic go-arounds less than 50ft of altitude will be lost. The gear is retracted once a positive rate of climb is achieved and the flaps are retracted as speed increases. Above 400ft, LNAV is selected to fly the routeing for the missed approach procedure.

Certainly one condition that would dictate a go-around is windshear — a sudden, rapid change in wind speed or direction typically found near thunderstorms but also caused by wind shifts around mountains, frontal activity and even buildings near the runway.

Windshear encounters are especially hazardous during take-off and landing when aircraft are low and slow and there is little time or altitude to recover. A crew may have as little as 5sec to recognise and react to a loss in airspeed and an increase in descent rate caused by windshear. It can overwhelm an aircraft's ability to climb with little or no advance warning, sometimes with deadly consequences. The most dangerous form of windshear is a microburst. This vertical column of wind, travelling downwards at speeds of up 160mph, descends much like water flowing from a tap — straight down but splashing out and up when it hits the ground.

In a typical windshear encounter, here is what pilots could expect: the aircraft first experiences a strong headwind from the outflow, causing an increase in airspeed and lift. If the crew do not suspect windshear, they lower the nose and reduce power to maintain the descent — the worst possible actions. The jet flies through the downdraught and encounters the outflow again but this time it is a tailwind which causes a sharp drop in airspeed and an increase in sink rate. The pilots have already reduced power and now are losing what lift they had left. A successful outcome depends on how swiftly and correctly they react to recover the lost airspeed. At the first sign of any large deviation in airspeed or vertical speed, pilots are trained to waste no time in initiating a go-around by 'aggressively' applying maximum thrust. The gear and flaps are left as they are until the shear is no longer a factor — opening the gear doors would increase drag. In a severe, low-altitude encounter, pilots are taught to trade airspeed for altitude, to increase pitch attitude though the airspeed may be dropping even to the point where the pilot is flying the jet on the edge of the stall with the stick shaker activated. Thankfully, better warning systems both on the ground and in the air and prudent flight planning to avoid conditions known to produce windshear make such encounters rare.

Moving along with the briefing, Kevin notes that the diversion airfield is Charlotte 227nm to the north but with good weather in the Atlanta area it appears unlikely they will need it.

Because both pilots are unfamiliar with the Atlanta airport, they pay close attention to the airport diagram, thinking ahead to the likely taxi route to the international terminal.

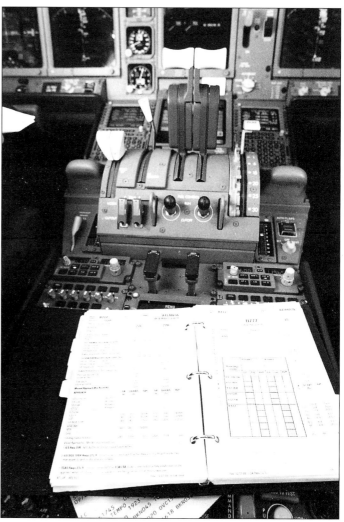

Elev	Var	A/D REF PT.	N33 38.4 W084 25.6	(W.B. HARTSFIELD) **ATLANTA**
1026	2°W			**AERODROME**

ATLANTA Clearance 121.65	**Ground** 121.9 (North) 121.75 (South)	**Tower** 119.5 119.1 (S)	**Departure** 125.7 (N) 125.0 (S)	**ATIS** 125.55 (Dep)	**VOT** 111.0	**D1** 01 JAN 98

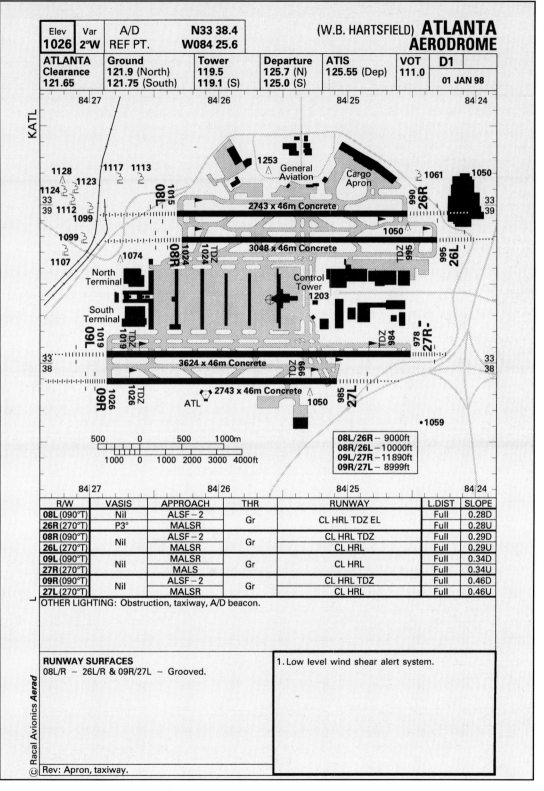

KATL

1253 ∧ General Aviation
Cargo Apron

2743 x 46m Concrete
3048 x 46m Concrete
3624 x 46m Concrete
2743 x 46m Concrete

North Terminal
South Terminal
Control Tower 1203

08L/26R — 9000ft
08R/26L — 10000ft
09L/27R — 11890ft
09R/27L — 8999ft

500 0 500 1000m
1000 0 1000 2000 3000 4000ft

ATL

R/W	VASIS	APPROACH	THR	RUNWAY	L.DIST	SLOPE
08L (090°T)	Nil	ALSF – 2	Gr	CL HRL TDZ EL	Full	0.28D
26R (270°T)	P3°	MALSR			Full	0.28U
08R (090°T)	Nil	ALSF – 2	Gr	CL HRL TDZ	Full	0.29D
26L (270°T)		MALSR		CL HRL	Full	0.29U
09L (090°T)	Nil	MALSR	Gr	CL HRL	Full	0.34D
27R (270°T)		MALS			Full	0.34U
09R (090°T)	Nil	ALSF – 2	Gr	CL HRL TDZ	Full	0.46D
27L (270°T)		MALSR		CL HRL	Full	0.46U

OTHER LIGHTING: Obstruction, taxiway, A/D beacon.

RUNWAY SURFACES
08L/R – 26L/R & 09R/27L – Grooved.

1. Low level wind shear alert system.

© Racal Avionics *Aerad*

Rev: Apron, taxiway.

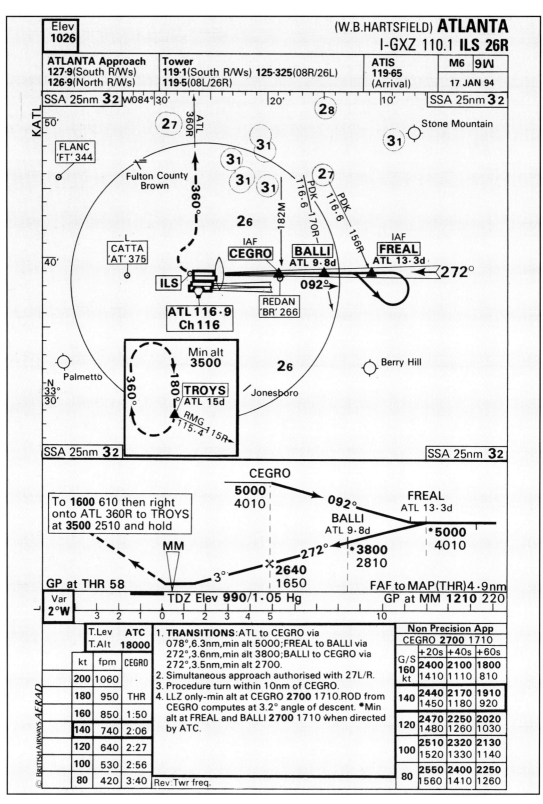

Though Kevin is the handling pilot, it will be Graeme who will fly the descent and initial approach before handing control back to Kevin just before touchdown. This airline procedure dates back to the practices of British European Airways. The philosophy behind it is to free the handling pilot from the task of flying the jet so he or she is better able to manage the approach and keep the big picture. If an autoland was planned, the handling pilot would resume 'control' at 1,000ft and manage the autopilot to landing. Today, however, Kevin plans a manual landing and will resume control of the aircraft on the approach when he is satisfied he can complete a visual landing. That could be at 1,000ft or on a bad weather day, right at minimums of 200ft.

At 19.26Z, a call from air traffic control ends the long stretch of cruise.

Atlanta Centre: 'Speedbird Seven November, Atlanta Centre descend and maintain flight level three one zero.'

Graeme dials up the new altitude on the mode control panel to initiate the descent. The aircraft starts down at Mach 0.784 and 750fpm. The flight is 150 miles northeast of the airport. Kevin takes advantage of the last few minutes of quiet to have a quick word with the passengers.

Captain PA: 'Ladies and gentlemen good afternoon, it's Captain Kevin Mottram once again. As you may have appreciated we have now started our descent into Atlanta. If we don't get any air traffic control delays, we should be landing in just twenty five minutes from now, well ahead of schedule. It's a rather busy time at Atlanta and we could find ourselves being held for a little while. If you haven't set your watches from the time in the UK, it's a matter of winding back five hours. Weather in Atlanta is fine, a rather cool afternoon, seven degrees Celsius, that's forty six degrees Fahrenheit. Thank you.'

The controller soon calls again and clears the flight to FL280. Through FL290, Kevin calls 'One to go' and at 19.34Z the jet levels at the assigned altitude.

The early arrival — a great way to end the inaugural run for the 777 — appears in jeopardy when a KLM flight ahead is given instructions to hold at the MACEY intersection, a waypoint northeast of the airport. Sure enough, it is not long before the controller is calling the British Airways flight.

Atlanta Centre: 'Speedbird Seven November is cleared to the MACEY intersection to hold northeast and probably expect further clearance at one niner five eight.'

It is not uncommon during busy periods or bad weather for arriving aircraft to wait out delays in a holding pattern. The aircraft fly a racetrack pattern around a radio beacon, or in this case a waypoint, until the controller can fit them into the landing pattern. The holding patterns themselves can get quite congested with each aircraft stacked at 1,000ft intervals, descending in stages as aircraft at the bottom of the stack are cleared from the hold for the approach. The controllers give the flight crews an estimate of how long they will be holding to assist with fuel planning. In this case, the crew have been told they will be holding for about 10min. Approaching MACEY, the jet is cleared to FL260, then down to 24,000ft. A transfer to a new controller brings welcome news — the hold has been cancelled.

Captain R/T: 'Atlanta, Speedbird Seven November level two six zero descending to level two four zero.'

Atlanta Centre: 'Speedbird Seven November, Atlanta Centre roger, resume normal speed and cross WOMAC intersection at and maintain one three thousand, two five zero knots, no holding, Atlanta altimeter two niner eight three.'

Through 20,000ft Graeme calls for the descent checklist: the decision height is checked displayed on the PFDs, autobrake set, Vref speed of 133kt confirmed displayed on the airspeed tape and the barometric pressure is set on both PFDs and the standby altimeter.

Atlanta Centre: 'Speedbird Seven November you're following a KLM seven six seven twelve o'clock and five miles out of fifteen five descending. Amend your altitude to maintain one six thousand please.'

The crew take a careful look out the front windshield and spot the KLM jet when the sun glints off its wing. The controller calls back a few minutes later with clearance to 14,000ft and asks the crew to slow to 250kt. Graeme pulls back on the speedbrake lever. Twelve of the 14 spoiler panels atop the wings rise into the airstream, creating drag and speeding the descent. At 310kt, the 777 can descend clean at about 2,300fpm and 5,500fpm with speedbrakes extended.

The autopilot is doing the physical work of guiding the aircraft to the airport, following the airspeed, heading and altitude instructions dialled into the mode control panel by the crew. The pilots though are alert to stay ahead of the jet in this busy airspace. They have to maintain situational awareness, a buzzword that means

RECEIVED FREE TEXT UPLINK MESSAGE

/.ATLKOBA.ATLANTA OPS
JUST TO FOREWARN YOU THAT WE HAVE A SPECIAL
WELCOME FOR YOU
YOU WILL BE DOUSED BY THE FIRE TRUCKS ON
ARRIVALS

Opposite:
The approach plate for the ILS to Runway 26 Right. *Racal Avionics*

Right:
The crew receive a datalink message from airline staff in Atlanta that hints at a special greeting awaiting the flight.

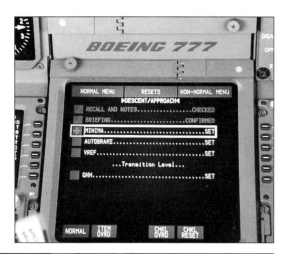

keeping a mental picture of the aircraft's position and altitude and where it is relative to the airport and other aircraft around them. At the same time, they have to keep a close ear on the nonstop radio chatter and plan their approach. The aircraft is transferred to Atlanta Approach on 127.9.

Captain R/T: 'Atlanta Approach, Speedbird Seven November passing one five thousand descending to one four thousand and we have Bravo.'

Atlanta Approach: 'Speedbird Seven November Atlanta Approach Control, expect runway two six right.'

The flight is now under the control of the approach controller who will vector the jet to within 30° to 40° of the runway centreline to intercept the ILS localiser. At a busy airport like Atlanta, approach controllers are masters at juggling aircraft as they organise arrivals from all directions into a neat, properly-spaced line-up for the runway.

Atlanta Approach control is located in a facility on the airport's east side and looks after the airspace within a 40-mile radius of the airport, surface to 14,000ft. It normally operates with four approach controllers and two final approach controllers. Also located in the facility is the traffic management unit which together with the Atlanta Air Route Traffic Control Centre regulates the flow of traffic in and out of Atlanta terminal airspace.

The frequency is busy as the controller fires off instructions nonstop to arriving aircraft, pausing only briefly to hear the pilots' replies: 'Delta fifteen Heavy, turn left one seven zero...Diamond one one Whiskey Foxtrot heading one seven zero, descend and maintain six thousand...Delta four eleven, turn left one niner zero...Delta four forty-three, do not reduce your speed, descend and maintain one two thousand...'

In the middle of this nonstop communication, Speedbird 7N is cleared to 10,000ft and given a right turn to 260° for spacing. They have been told to expect a landing on Runway 26 Right. Since this is different from what the crew planned for, Kevin makes the necessary changes to the FMC and the new ILS frequency is automatically tuned.

Airspace around big US airports is very congested and late descent clearances and requests to keep the speed up are common so crews have to guard against unstable, rushed approaches. Graeme has a few rules of thumb to assist with approach planning. At 30nm from the field, he likes to be at 9,000ft or lower and slowed to less than 250kt. At 20nm, he wants to be below 6,000ft and flying no faster than 220kt with flaps starting to be deployed. A sleek design and a very efficient wing make the 777 a tough aircraft to slow. It requires about 65sec and 6nm to slow from 310kt to 250kt and takes almost another minute and 4nm to slow to the flaps-up manoeuvring speed, roughly about 200kt at landing weights.

The radio crackles with instructions to turn back left to 190°. Further instructions put the flight on a heading of 180° and clear it down to 6,000ft. As requested, the jet has slowed to 250kt, the maximum speed below 10,000ft in the United States.

Above:
Graeme eases back on the speedbrake lever... and spoiler panels on the wings rise into the airstream to increase drag and speed descent.

Above right:
'Speedbird Seven November turn left one niner zero.' The jet turns to its new heading.
John M. Dibbs

Control of the flight is passed to the final approach controller on 118.35. Kevin checks in passing 8,000ft.

Atlanta Approach: 'Speedbird Seven November, descend and maintain 5,000 and you can go ahead and reduce to one eight zero now.'

The controller wants the 777 to both descend and slow down. To meet the request, Graeme pulls the speedbrake lever back to add more drag. The descent rate increases to nearly 2,000fpm and the airspeed begins to drop. Out the window, the Georgian countryside has given way to city suburbs with their residential subdivisions and blocks of industrial land. Through 5,500ft Graeme calls 'Flap 1'. The airspeed tape automatically shows the maximum speed for each flap setting. Kevin ensures the speed is within 20kt of 193kt, the speed limit for this flap setting, and moves the flap lever back a notch. At Flap 1, only the slats move, deploying to a mid-range position. If the aircraft is going too fast for the selected flap setting, a feature called flap load relief prevents them from being deployed until the speed is slowed to the proper range. Likewise, if the 777 accelerates past the safe flap extension speed, the flaps will retract and then redeploy as the jet slows again.

Atlanta Approach: 'Speedbird Seven November, turn to heading two five zero, join localiser for runway two six right.'

The new heading is dialled up and the 777 banks towards the airport. In the turn, Graeme presses APP on the mode control panel, arming the three autopilots to capture the localiser and glideslope. LOC and GS appear on the top of each PFD, informing the crew the autopilots are ready to intercept the ILS. Graeme also calls for Flap 5 which extends the trailing edge flaps. The flaps — moved by hydraulic power against the stiff resistance of the airflow — extend from the back of the wing to increase its surface area and angle downward to increase the curve of the wing. The slats extend forward and down from the front of the wing. By working in this fashion, flaps and slats help the wing create more lift, allowing the aircraft to fly slower for the approach.

On the PFDs, the localiser needle is seen moving to the centre of the display, indicating the aircraft is nearing the extended centreline of the runway. However, the controller has turned the flight too late for a successful intercept and the jet passes through the localiser. It flies a series of S-turns before settling on the localiser 15nm from the runway. The aircraft is level at 5,000ft when it intercepts the glideslope passing FREAL, the initial approach fix 13.3nm back on the approach. Flap 15 is selected as the autopilot starts the aircraft down to the runway at 900fpm. The missed approach altitude of 3,500ft is selected in the altitude window of the mode control panel.

Atlanta Approach: 'Speedbird Seven November, your traffic is 12 o'clock, five ahead now. Do you have the airport in sight?'

Captain R/T: 'We have the airport but not the aircraft.'

Above:
The First Officer rests his hand lightly on the throttles as the engines retard to idle thrust during the descent.

Right:
The controller turns the flight to 180° and clears it down to 6,000ft. Graeme makes the selections on the mode control panel.

Below:
Passing 9,000ft, the flight is on an extended right base leg for Runway 26 Right. The ND displays FREAL, the initial approach fix, and 5,000, the altitude the jet should be at when it passes the waypoint. Also displayed is the missed approach procedure which is a right turn to the TROYS waypoint north of the airport where the jet would hold to await further clearance. TCAS shows numerous other aircraft in the area.

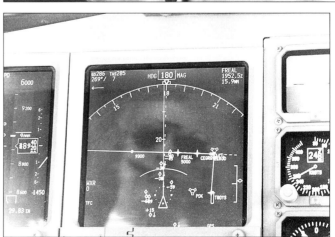

Atlanta Approach: 'Speedbird Seven November, you're cleared the visual approach two six right, reduce speed to one six zero.'

The runway is visible ahead — 9,000ft of concrete, its touchdown zone stained black from the rubber deposits left by the countless arrivals that have preceded 'Seven November'.

Through 3,500ft Graeme calls for the gear. Kevin leans across the flightdeck and moves the gear selector down. A loud thunk and the rush of air is heard as the nose gear drops out of its well into the slipstream. Kevin checks the EICAS for indications that the nose and main gear are down and locked. With the speedbrake armed and cabin reported ready for arrival, the landing checklist is completed. Descending along the 3° glideslope, the jet is pitched about 1° nose up.

The radio altimeter comes alive at 2,500ft and an automated female voice calls out, 'radio altimeter'.

Flap 20 is selected, followed quickly by Flap 30 and the speed slows to 152kt. With Flap 25 or 30 selected, the leading edge slats extend further forward to a gapped position. The jet vibrates from the extra aerodynamic drag as the flaps move further back. With the selection of landing flaps, the engines also idle at a higher speed to reduce the spool-up time in case full power is required for a go-around.

The final approach speed of 138kt — Vref + 5kt — is selected in the IAS window of the mode control panel and the power reduces slightly to slow the jet to the new speed.

At 800ft and less than a minute to touchdown, Kevin resumes control of the aircraft. A loud 'Whoop, Whoop' of the master warning alarm sounds on the flightdeck as he cancels the autopilot and takes over for a manual landing. Staying centred on the localiser and glideslope requires constant small movements of the control column. With Kevin flying the jet, Graeme resumes handling the radios and he checks in with the tower six miles back on the ILS.

First Officer R/T: 'Tower, Speedbird Seven November Heavy fully established two six right.'

Atlanta Tower: 'Speedbird Seven November Heavy, Atlanta Tower good afternoon. You're following a Boeing seven six seven, caution wake turbulence, runway two six right, cleared to land.'

At 50ft above the decision height the automated voice calls '50 Above' and then 'Decide'. Kevin responds 'Land', confirming that he is continuing with the landing.

Almost immediately, the speed begins to drop unexpectedly. Kevin reaches to the glareshield and dials in a few extra knots on the airspeed window for the

Top:
As the aircraft turns onto the final approach, Graeme presses APP on the mode control panel, arming the three autopilots to capture the localiser and glideslope.

Above:
Flying the ILS. Just 2.5nm back from the runway, the jet is descending through 1,800ft at 144kt, nicely aligned on the glideslope and localiser. The circle in upper right of the PFD is the readout from the radio altimeter and indicates height above ground.

autothrottle. The speed drops more sharply to 128kt, 10kt below the approach speed, and it is now clear the aircraft has hit windshear. The autothrottle is adding power but not fast enough. Graeme, who has been monitoring the instruments since handing over control, drops his hand to the throttles to increase thrust but Kevin is already pushing the levers forward, giving the aircraft a burst of power.

The aircraft flies through the other side of the downdraught where it encounters a tailwind. That and the extra power make the jet a little fast, causing it to float for a short bit over the runway.

Left:
At 800ft, Kevin cancels the autopilot and takes control of the jet for a manual landing. He uses small movements of the control column to remain on the glideslope and localiser.

Above:
As the aircraft exits the runway, Graeme reaches to the overhead panel to turn on the APU and at the Captain's cue proceeds with the After Landing checklist.

Right:
An airport fire truck stands ready to douse the aircraft.

Landing a Boeing 777 is made easier by a generous ground effect, essentially a cushion of air caught between the runway and the plane's big wing and large flaps. This helps arrest the descent rate in the final feet before touchdown.

The automated voice has continued the altitude call-outs down to landing: '100, 50, 30, 20' and '10'.

At 25ft, the autothrottle retards the power to idle thrust. Kevin raises the nose slightly, just a degree or two, to flare the aircraft. At the normal touchdown attitude of 4° to 5°, the aft body clearance is about 55in.

The touchdown is smooth as the main wheels kiss the pavement with a screech of rubber and a cloud of blue smoke. The spoiler panels automatically rise from the top of the wing, killing the wing's ability to create lift and putting the weight of the jet firmly on the main gear for better braking. Kevin releases some of the back pressure on the control column, allowing the nosewheel to touch the runway.

Graeme pulls the reverser levers — located on the front of the throttles — up and back to the reverse idle interlock position. The cowling on each engine moves back to block the fan exhaust and deflect it forward. On the EICAS 'REV' appears in amber above the engine indications to confirm the cowlings are in transit, and then green when in position. Confirming the cowlings have deployed, Graeme pulls the throttles further back to select full reverse thrust and a roar is heard as power increases.

The jet slows as reverse thrust bites the air and autobraking takes effect. At 60kt, power is reduced to reverse idle to avoid blowing debris in front of the engines where it could be ingested by the huge fans. At taxying speed, Kevin calls for 'forward idle' power and, using the sidewall tiller, steers the aircraft on to the Bravo 3 taxiway, about 6,900ft down the runway.

First Officer R/T: 'Speedbird Seven November vacated on Bravo Three for [gate] Echo 33.'

Atlanta Tower: 'Speedbird Seven November Heavy, make the left turn there and proceed eastbound on taxiway Bravo.'

As the jet enters the taxiway, Kevin moves the speedbrake lever ahead to retract the spoiler panels. That is Graeme's cue to proceed with the After Landing checks: the flaps are retracted, landing and strobe lights are turned OFF; the autothrottle selected to OFF; weather radar is checked OFF; the autobrake is turned OFF. Graeme reaches to the overhead panel and rotates the APU knob to START and releases it. The APU automatically starts and its generator comes on line to supply electricity to aircraft systems after engine shutdown.

The crew are matter-of-fact about the small drama on short final. Although it was not a serious windshear encounter, fast action was required to spare the jet a jarring bump on the runway.

Above:
A traditional airport greeting welcomes the jet to mark the inaugural flight of a British Airways 777 to Atlanta.
Atlanta Journal-Constitution/David Tulis

The tower asks the crew to hold short of Runway 26 Left. A departing Delta 727 thunders off the parallel runway and the British Airways jet is cleared to the ramp.

Atlanta Tower: 'Speedbird Seven November Heavy, cross two six left, south on Dixie into six north between the fire trucks.'

Pilots rarely want to be greeted by airport fire crews after landing. However, on this day a dash of Southern hospitality rather than an emergency has brought the trucks from their hall. It is a traditional airport greeting, in this case to celebrate the inaugural run of the 777 to Hartsfield. Two fire trucks have positioned themselves at the entrance to the tarmac and as the jet passes between them, they douse it with streams of water pumped from their turrets.

A cluster of news photographers and camera crews have gathered at the gate. The first scheduled flight of a Boeing 777 into Atlanta has attracted some media attention.

Approaching the stand, Graeme makes the PA call, 'Cabin crew, doors to manual', a reminder to the crew to disarm the doors. Needless to say, it would be a bit embarrassing to have the 777 featured on the six o'clock news with an accidentally deployed emergency escape chute blowing in the wind. The ground crew can be seen preparing the variety of equipment needed to unload and service the aircraft once it has docked.

Kevin guides the aircraft smoothly onto the yellow line leading to the gate. At the designated spot, he stops the jet and sets the parking brake. It has taken just 6min to get from the runway to the terminal. The crew confirm electricity is flowing from the APU, then move the fuel control switches to CUTOFF to shut down the engines. The loading bridge is moved into position and the cabin door opened.

Left:
At the gate, the engines are turned off and the crew proceed with the shutdown checklist.

Above:
Atlanta's Hartsfield airport is the main hub for Delta Air Lines and the airline is by far its biggest user with 1,200 arrivals and departures a day. Delta has ordered 10 777s with Trent 892 engines to be delivered between August 1999 and December 2000.

Left:
In just a few short hours 'India Juliet' will be airborne again with a new crew, winging its way back to England and Gatwick Airport.

It is 20.07Z. British Airways Flight 2227 is in Atlanta after a flight of 8hr 52min and a gate-to-gate time of 9hr 10min. The upper EICAS shows 8.6 tonnes of fuel remaining — 1,100kg above the required reserves. Total fuel burn was 59.7 tonnes. Remarkably, the flight time was just 1min off the flightplan and the fuel remaining is exactly what the crew expected.

The crew quickly run through the shutdown checks, turning off the hydraulic pumps, fuel pumps and beacon lights. Kevin jots a few entries in the technical log for the benefit of the next crew.

The passengers are quick to exit the cabin, all of them anxious to complete their journey whether it is to a downtown hotel for a business visit, home to see family or perhaps catching another flight to a final destination. The cabin — temporary home to 152 passengers for more than 9hr — is empty now. Newspapers, magazines, rumpled blankets and pillows litter the vacant seats. In the few hours before the jet departs again for Gatwick, a team of cleaners will sweep through the cabin, tidying it up for the next load of travellers and the galleys will be re-stocked with dinners, snacks and beverages.

The flight crew and cabin staff make their way through customs and immigration and take an escalator to the bottom level of the concourse. Here they can walk, step on a travelator or board Atlanta's unique shuttle trains to the main terminal. These automatic trains — with a capacity to move 128,000 passengers an hour — run at 100sec intervals between the five concourses and the terminal building.

A bus takes the crew on a 45min drive to their hotel. Despite the late hour for most of them — it is going on 11pm London time — most will nip over to a nearby mall and then out for some supper before turning in for the night.

Tomorrow evening, they will be on duty once more as the crew of British Airways Flight 2226, the return flight to Gatwick.

Appendix I. Flightplan

British Airways Flight 2227 from London Gatwick to Hartsfield Atlanta International Airport

BOEING 777-236 INCREASED GROSS WEIGHT, G-VIIJ

Stage length	3,855nm
Block time	9hr 10min
Airborne time	8hr 52min
Take-off weight	252,472kg
V1/VR/V2	148/148/153
Total fuel	68.3 tonnes
Cruising altitude	FL370, climbing to FL390 after the ocean crossing
Cruise level temperature	-65° Celsius
Cruise level winds	261° @ 50kt at ocean's midpoint
TAS/Mach	490kt/Mach 0.842
Fuel burn	3.6 tonnes per engine per hour
En route alternates	Manchester and Goose Bay
Landing alternate	Charlotte, North Carolina
Vref	133kt
Landing weight	193,400kg
Fuel burned	59.7 tonnes
Fuel left on arrival	8.6 tonnes

POSITION	NAVAID	ROUTE	TIME	LEG DIST	TOTAL DIST
Gatwick R/W 26L	-	SID	0	10	10
Gatwick	NDB	SID	.04	5	15
MID-067	WPT	SID	.05	8	23
MIDHURST	VOR	SID	.06	28	51
SOUTHAMPTON	VOR	UR8	.11	46	97
GIBSO	WPT	UR14	.18	41	138
EXMOR	WPT	UR14	.23	17	155
Top of Climb	-	UR14	.25	20	175
SWANY	WPT	UR14	.28	43	218
STRUMBLE	VOR	UR14	.33	38	256
VATRY	WPT	UR14	.38	64	320
DUBLIN	VOR	UN560	.46	61	381
ERNAN	WPT	UN550	.54	100	481
5510N	WPT	NAT F	1.07	356	837
5720N	WPT	NAT F	1.55	339	1,176
5930N	WPT	NAT F	2.42	309	1,485
5940N	WPT	NAT F	3.25	339	1,824
5750N	WPT	NAT F	4.13	250	2,074
LOACH	WPT	NAT F	4.49	100	2,174
FOXXE	WPT	DCT	5.03	200	2,374
GOLFE	WPT	DCT	5.30	261	2,635
BAIE-COMEAU	VOR	DCT	6.05	99	2,734
RIVIÈRE DU LOUP	VOR	DCT	6.18	349	3,083
ALBANY	VOR	J6	7.04	76	3,159
FLOSI	WPT	J6	7.14	30	3,189
SPARTA	VOR	J6	7.18	21	3,210
BROADWAY	VOR	J77	7.20	48	3,258
POTTSTOWN	VOR	J48	7.27	34	3,292
PENSY	WPT	J48	7.31	44	3,336
WESTMINISTER	VOR	J48	7.37	66	3,402
CASANOVA	VOR	J48	7.45	73	3,475
MONTEBELLO	VOR	J48	7.55	78	3,553
JOINN	VOR	J48	8.05	159	3,712
Top of Descent	-	J48	8.25	42	3,754
FOOTHILLS	VOR	STAR	8.31	29	3,783
MACEY	WPT	STAR	8.35	16	3,799
WOMAC	WPT	STAR	8.38	11	3,810
LOGEN	WPT	STAR	8.40	29	3,839
ATLANTA R/W 26R	-	ATC	8.46	16	3,855

	209ft 1in
	199ft 11in
t	60ft 9in
ge diameter	20ft 4in
bin cross-section	19ft 3in

PERFORMANCE DATA

TAKE-OFF

Maximum take-off weight	267,619kg
Maximum zero fuel weight	195,044kg
Passengers	267
Take-off field length	9,700ft (sea level, 86° F)
Take-off thrust	84,700lb per engine

CRUISE

Cruise Mach	0.84
Maximum Mach	0.87
Ceiling at MTOW	34,700ft
Max certificated ceiling	43,100ft

LANDING

Maximum landing weight	208,652kg
Approach speed @ MLW	138kt
Landing field length	5,200ft

SYSTEMS

HYDRAULICS

Number of independent systems	Three
Number of independent pumps	Nine
System pressure	3,000psi
Type of pumps	Two engine-driven
	Four electrical
	Two air-driven
	RAT pump

ELECTRICAL POWER

Number of ac generators	Six
Location and capacity	Engine
	2 @ 120kVA
	2 back-up @ 20VA
	APU 120kVA
	RAT 7.5kVA
Transformer rectifier units	Five

AUXILIARY POWER UNIT

Model	AlliedSignal Engines 331-500
Operational altitudes	Pneumatic power to 22,000ft
	Electrical power to 43,100ft
Maximum in-flight start altitude	43,100ft